SHORT CUTS

INTRODUCTIONS TO FILM STUDIES

T0324452

SHORT CUTS

INTRODUCTIONS TO FILM STUDIES

FOR A COMPLETE LIST OF TITLES IN THE SERIES, PLEASE SEE PAGES 159–160

THE CONTEMPORARY SUPERHERO FILM

PROJECTIONS OF POWER AND IDENTITY

TERENCE McSWEENEY

WALLFLOWER

NEW YORK

Wallflower Press is an imprint of Columbia University Press
Publishers Since 1893
New York   Chichester, West Sussex
cup.columbia.edu

Library of Congress Cataloging-in-Publication Data

Names: McSweeney, Terence, 1974- author.
Title: The contemporary superhero film : projections of power and identity
   / Terence McSweeney.
Description: New York : Wallfower Press, 2020. I Series: Short cuts I
   Includes bibliographical references and index.
Identifiers: LCCN 2020011038 (print) I LCCN 2020011039 (ebook) I
   ISBN 9780231192415 (trade paperback) I ISBN 9780231549790 (ebook)
Subjects: LCSH: Superhero films—History and criticism. I
   Comic strip characters in motion pictures. I Comic books, strips, etc—
   United States—Film adaptations.
Classification: LCC PN1995.9.S76 M37 2020 (print) I
   LCC PN1995.9.S76 (ebook) I DDC 791.43/652—dc23
LC record available at https://lccn.loc.gov/2020011038
LC ebook record available at https://lccn.loc.gov/2020011039

Cover image: Warner Bros./Photofest

Dedicated to Matt, David, Ben, Jason, Alison, Ruth, Jane, Rachel and Dan: 1992–1995

CONTENTS

ACKNOWLEDGMENTS

This project has been one of the most pleasurable of my writing career, and it is a wonderful privilege to join the ranks of those who have contributed to the Short Cuts series. My thanks go to Yoram Allon for making it happen and Ryan Groendyk for seeing it through to the end. I was very fortunate to be able to write this book at a time when interest in the superhero film has never been greater, which gave me the opportunity to present many of my ideas at a range of locations, both within the academic sphere and, just as importantly, outside of it. Thank you to the British Film Institute for the invitation to speak to the public (alongside my colleague Dr. Claire Hines) as part of their New Writings series in December 2018. I would also like to thank the wonderful staff and students at my own institution, Solent University (especially Dr. Stuart Joy) and those at the Lilly Library, Indiana University, where I was lucky enough to be the recipient of their generous Everett Helm Fellowship. The archives at the Lilly Library provided an invaluable insight into the tapestry of the history of the United States, which formed and continues to sustain the superhero phenomenon. Finally, to my loving family: to a father who nurtured my love for film, a mother for all her help and support over the years, and the three people who are the inspiration for all it is that I do, Olga, Harrison, and Wyatt, to whom this book is dedicated with love.

THE CONTEMPORARY
SUPERHERO FILM

INTRODUCTION

Cultural Phenomenon or Cultural Catastrophe?

You will give the people an ideal to strive towards. They will race behind you, they will stumble, they will fall. But in time, they will join you in the sun. In time, you will help them accomplish wonders. . . .

—Jor-El in *Man of Steel* (2013)

The immense popularity of live action superhero adaptations, and Hollywood's relatively recent embrace of comic book characters, reflects a shifting range of cultural, political, economic, industrial and technological issues. . . . Despite the assumption often made by film critics, viewers and even some of the film-makers that superhero movies are merely simple-minded and juvenile entertainment (derived from silly and childish comic books), there is no simple answer for why this genre is so appealing at this moment in history. . . .

—Jeffrey A. Brown, *The Modern Superhero in Film and Television: Popular Genre and American Culture* (2016)

In April 2019 *Avengers: Endgame*, the twenty-second film in what is widely referred to as the MCU (Marvel Cinematic Universe), smashed box-office records all over the globe on its way to becoming the most financially successful film ever made, almost exactly eleven years after the first film in the series, *Iron Man*, in 2008. Given the unprecedented financial success and cultural impact of the MCU, a franchise that has made billions of dollars at the cinema and many billions more in other subsidiary revenue streams outside of it on its way to becoming the largest film franchise in the history of the medium, it is hard to recall what a gamble *Iron Man* once was for the then fledgling film studio. During the 1990s and early 2000s Marvel had grown increasingly dissatisfied with licensing its iconic characters out to other studios and decided to make the move into film production, where the financial risks are undoubtedly greater but so are the potential rewards. When *Iron Man* went into production what some have subsequently referred to as the superhero "renaissance," "resurgence," "boom," "rebirth," or "revival" had yet to entirely solidify, but within a few years the superhero film would become the most popular genre for audiences around the world.[1] Indeed, 2008 is the year Liam Burke argues should be regarded as the time "the superhero movie and comic book movie genres arguably found their 'real voice.'"[2] This "real voice" that Burke speaks of is demonstrated by the fact that for the first time ever in 2008 there were three superhero films in the top ten global box office: *The Dark Knight*, *Iron Man*, and *Hancock*, with the former making more than a billion dollars worldwide and winning two of the eight Academy Awards it was nominated for (Best Supporting Actor and Best Sound Editing). Ten years later in 2018, the genre had consolidated this position of global box-office superiority and acute cultural impact with not only its first ever Best Picture nomination at the Academy Awards for *Black Panther*, but a remarkable six out of the top ten most financially successful films of the year featured superheroes: *Avengers: Infinity War*, *Black Panther*, *Incredibles 2*, *Venom*, *Deadpool 2*, and *Aquaman* (with *Ant-Man and the Wasp* just outside at number eleven). This was an unprecedented feat for any genre in the history of the medium and contributed significantly to 2018 being the highest earning year in box office history in both the United States (with a total of $11.85 billion) and globally ($41.7 billion) at that time.[3] The following year in 2019 *Avengers: Endgame* was, of course, expected to be successful, but it was even bigger than anyone could have anticipated, even Kevin Feige himself, president of Marvel Studios and the architect of Marvel's transition from comic book publisher to veteran film studio, with an opening weekend of $357 million at the domestic box office, a full $100 million more than the record set in the previous year by *Avengers: Infinity War*, and an international gross of more than a billion dollars in three days, two feats that had never even come close to being achieved before. The film ultimately passed James Cameron's *Avatar* (2009) as the most successful film ever made, with a gross of over $2.79 billion.

It was not always like this. Superheroes have been a perennial part of popular culture since the appearance of Superman (April 1938), Batman (May 1939), Captain America (March 1941), and Wonder Woman (October 1941) in the first editions of their respective comic books, and had intermittently reached the television and cinema screens in the subsequent decades. But while the 1970s and 1980s saw the groundbreaking release of *Superman* (1978) and Tim Burton's *Batman* (1989), both of which began hugely successful, long-running franchises and inspired generations of children to play with action figures, eat from branded lunchboxes, and sleep on pillow cases adorned with their heroes' faces, they did not inspire the wave of additions to the genre the likes of which we have experienced since the turn of the millennium that are the focus of this book.

Like most cultural and artistic moments, the return of superhero genre, whether we wish to call it a renaissance or a resurgence or use some other, much more pejorative term as some critics have, proves difficult to date. Liam Burke is right to say that by 2008 it had found it's "real voice," but a case can be made that this return actually started as early Bryan Singer's *X-Men* (2000), which earned a then formidable $296 million dollars and was the only superhero film in the top ten global box office, indeed the only notable American superhero film even made in that year. *X-Men* revealed to studios that there was money to be made again in the genre after the excesses of the late 1980s and 1990s had seen both the Superman and Batman franchises devour themselves in the wake of the critical and commercial disappointments of their respective fourth installments, *Superman IV: Quest for Peace* (1987) and *Batman & Robin* (1997). Might we instead consider Sam Raimi's *Spider-Man* (2002), made two years later, as the true starting point? The film not only reinvented the character in his first real big screen appearance but also unquestionably established a template for the majority of superhero films that followed, and it was the first film from the genre to be the highest grossing film of the year at the domestic box office since *Batman* in 1989. What, though, of Christopher Nolan's richly textured *Batman Begins* (2005), a film that arguably approached the superhero genre *seriously* for the first time and began an influential trilogy which would redefine it in a process that has been described by some as "Nolanisation"?[4] Each of these three films, while certainly not realistic in the sense the term is usually applied to cinema, set their narratives in more believable worlds, with more human protagonists than those that appeared in the genre in the decades before. In the modern superhero film characters tend not to fly around the world to turn back time to return a loved one to life, as Superman once did in *Superman* or pick up the Statue of Liberty, as he did in *Superman IV: The Quest for Peace*. Contemporary superhero films do not usually have scenes like the brilliantly exaggerated art gallery heist in *Batman*, orchestrated to Prince's "Partyman" (1989), or armies of penguins equipped with rockets like those in *Batman Returns* (1992). Far from this, as David Goyer, the screenwriter of *Batman Begins* and *Man of Steel* suggested, the new superhero films are those which "could happen in the same world in which we live."[5]

While its commercial and cultural impact is impossible to deny, the genre has been frequently criticized throughout its history, as early as Fredric Wertham's now much derided *Seduction of the Innocent* (1954). In more recent years these criticisms have been wide ranging: Academy Award winning director Alejandro González Iñárritu remarked of the superhero genre, "They have been poison, this cultural genocide, because the audience is so overexposed to plot and explosions and shit that doesn't say anything about the experience of being human."[6] Jodie Foster continued the environmental disaster metaphor when she informed the *Radio Times* that "studios making bad content in order to appeal to the masses and shareholders is like fracking—you get the best return right now but you wreck the earth. It's ruining the viewing habits of the American population and then ultimately the rest of the world."[7] And the renowned graphic novelist Alan Moore declared they were to be considered a "cultural catastrophe."[8] There is a pronounced element of elitism embodied in many of these comments about the genre, which can be seen even more explicitly in those by Ethan Hawke, an Academy Award–nominated actor (*Training Day* [2001] and *Boyhood* [2014]), who stated, "Now we have the problem that they tell us *Logan* [2017] is a great movie. Well, it's a great superhero movie. It still involves people in tights with metal coming out of their hands. It's not [Robert] Bresson. It's not [Ingmar] Bergman,"[9] a sentiment that is frequently combined with the contention that the genre is one only suitable for children, with adults who express their appreciation of it found guilty of being deficient in some way. Two notable directors who each made their mark on the science fiction film in the second half of the twentieth century asserted this quite clearly: David Cronenberg, who said, "A superhero movie, by definition, you know, it's comic book. It's for kids," and Terry Gilliam, who stated, "I hate superheroes. It's bullshit. Come on, grow up!".[10] Susan Faludi, in her essential *The Terror Dream: Fear and Fantasy in the Post-9/11 Era* (2007), argued that the superhero only appeals to "someone, typically a prepubescent teenage boy, who feels weak in the world and insufficient to the demands of the day and who needs a Walter Mitty bellows to pump up his self-worth."[11] Cronenberg, Gilliam, and Faludi insist that there is little of worth to be found for adults in the superhero genre, an assumption that the box office numbers and audience statistics might be seen to challenge. In the case of the record-breaking opening weekend of *Avengers: Endgame* in the United States. audiences were reportedly made up of 57 percent male and 43 percent female; of those only 11 percent were teens, with 71 percent being adults.[12]

These criticisms came to a head in 2019, the very same year the genre had achieved such unprecedented financial success and cultural impact, with esteemed director Martin Scorsese's comments describing superhero films, in particular those from the MCU, as "not cinema. Honestly, the closest I can think of them, as well-made as they are, with actors doing the best they can under the circumstances, is theme parks. It isn't the cinema of human beings trying to convey emotional, psychological experiences to another human being."[13] Scorsese's criticisms, which he expanded upon in a thought-provoking follow-up article in the *New York Times*, undeniably raised valid points about the ubiquity of franchise films and their hold over what audiences are offered at the cinema. Of course, if anyone has earned the right to an opinion about the American film industry it is certainly Martin Scorsese, yet his assertion emerges as problematic with the admission that he *had never actually seen* a superhero film all the way to the end. To level such unqualified opprobrium at something one has never experienced is just as questionable as those who picketed Scorsese's own *The Last Temptation of Christ* (1988) without viewing it.[14] A more reasonable suggestion, one that can be applied to any film regardless of the genre it contributes to, might be to use the approach suggested by the cinematographer Dante Spinotti. The renowned Italian director of photography has worked on a superhero film, *Ant-Man and the Wasp* (2018), but is more famous for the two Academy Award nominations he received for Curtis Hanson's *L.A Confidential* (1997) and Michael Mann's *The Insider* (1999). In the wake of Scorsese's comments Spinotti remarked, "I divide movie-making into two large categories good movies and bad movies. That's all there is to it."[15] Simply put there are good superhero films and bad superhero films, just as there are good and bad horror films, westerns, musicals, biopics, and gangster films—where the majority of Scorsese's oeuvre resides. To state that all entrants from any given genre are not worthy of being called "cinema" is both illogical and misguided. George Miller, Scorsese's contemporary and a director who has worked in more genres than most but not yet made a superhero film, commented, "To be honest, in terms of this debate, cinema is cinema and it's a very broad church. The test, ultimately, is what it means to the audience."[16]

It might be hard to convince these numerous critics of the pleasures and cultural relevance of the superhero genre, but it has not been hard to do the same for the public, which has gone to see them in droves in an age when cinema attendance is down across the board, even though studios earn higher profits than ever. Yet ultimately this is the central purpose of this slim volume in the Short Cuts series: to open up avenues of discussion for the genre's efficacy and its relevance, its possibilities and

Fig. 0.1 The superhero film as the most popular genre around the globe: Catastrophe or phenomenon? The record-breaking *Avengers: Endgame* (2019).

limitations, and, ultimately, its cultural importance. This book argues that the genre is worth studying not despite the criticisms directed at it but because of them, and not simply due to its financial success but also for a diverse variety of reasons, the first of which might be that it alone, above all genres, has come to embody and even redefine the parameters of the contemporary Hollywood blockbuster film, providing a template for many of the changes that have swept through the industry over the last twenty years. This is an era that has seen the embrace of CGI (computer generated images), action, and spectacle, leading to what has been described by some as a return to the "cinema of attractions," Tom Gunning's categorization of trends in the early decades of cinema history that sought to directly solicit "spectator attention, inciting visual curiosity, and supplying pleasure through an exciting spectacle—a unique event."[17]

Until quite recently sequels were generally expected to generate diminishing returns for studios and almost always less critical praise. As Carolyn Jess-Cooke wrote in her *Film Sequels: Theory and Practice from Hollywood to Bollywood* (2009), "The reason why a sequel disappoints—and why the very concept of sequelisation is met with a collective groan—seems to do with how the sequel re-imagines and extends the source in ways than impose upon our memories and interpretation of the previous film. In creating a second ending of an 'original' the sequel conjures a previous viewing experience, and it is precisely this imposition of spectatorial memory, or this kind of enforced retro-interpretation and continuation, that appears to underline the sense of dissatisfaction that the sequel often creates."[18] This was the commonly held view before 2009, when Jess-Cooke's book was published, illustrated by the diminishing financial and critical returns of the original incarnations of franchises like Superman (1978–1987), Batman (1989–1997), and the Beverly Hills Cop trilogy (1984–1994). Yet in the modern era this is far from the case, with sequels now expected to earn more money than the films that precede them, both inside and outside of the superhero genre. Indeed, the sequel paradigm which defined Hollywood film production from the 1980s to the early 2000s is now seen as progressively outdated for more substantial brands in an age where the "universe" model is considered a more compatible long-term business strategy. This model can be very lucrative, fueling as it does a linked chain of additional revenue streams, from toys and video games to music and theme park rides, but it can also collapse: as ambitious plans to follow the likes of *X-Men Origins: Wolverine* (2009), *The Amazing Spider-Man* (2012), *Ghostbusters* (2016), *The Mummy* (2017), and *King Arthur: Legend of the Sword* (2017) disappeared after their first installments failed to meet the expectations of either producers or fans.[19] These developments, propelled to a large extent by the superhero film, have led to the emergence of new terminology required to keep up with these changes. Prior to 2000s the word "sequel" seemed to be just about enough to describe what came after a financially successful film if producers decided to make another installment (and sometimes "prequel"), but now audiences have become increasingly familiar with terms like reboot, reimagining, sidequel, midquel, interquel, paraquel, circumquel, and even stealth sequel![20]

The superhero genre also provides us with the consummate example of the increasing size, speed, and frequency of blockbuster scale film production. For example, prior to this contemporary revival of the genre, the Batman franchise in the late 1980s and 1990s comprised of four films released over a nine-year period: *Batman* (1989), *Batman Returns* (1992), *Batman Forever* (1995), and *Batman & Robin* (1997). Superman followed exactly the same pattern: *Superman* (1978), *Superman II* (1980), *Superman III* (1983),

Fig. 0.2 The superhero genre exemplifies the American film industry's transition from the dominance of the sequel to the universe model in films like *Batman v Superman: Dawn of Justice* (2016), where three iconic figures share the screen for the first time ever.

and *Superman IV: The Quest for Peace* (1987). However, as we have seen, phases 1, 2, and 3 of the MCU consisted of twenty-three films in the space of eleven years, with Robert Downey Jr. playing Iron Man/Tony Stark in ten of these: *Iron Man* (2008), *The Incredible Hulk* (2008), *Iron Man 2* (2010), *The Avengers* (2012), *Iron Man 3* (2013), *Avengers: Age of Ultron* (2015), *Captain America: Civil War* (2016), *Spider-Man: Homecoming* (2017), *Avengers: Infinity War* (2018), and *Avengers: End Game* (2019)—more than the combined appearances of Batman and Superman in both their aforementioned franchises—and even in five blockbusters across five successive summers. Furthermore, the speed with which the reboot process now moves is also remarkable; thus, a mere five years after the conclusion of Raimi's Spider-Man trilogy (2002–2007) the character was rebooted and recast, played by Andrew Garfield in two films directed by Marc Webb: *The Amazing Spider-Man* (2012) and *The Amazing Spider-Man 2* (2014); which was followed just two years later when the character was brought into the Marvel Cinematic Universe after an agreement was reached between Sony and Marvel; this time played by Tom Holland, first as part of an ensemble in *Captain America: Civil War* (2016), then in his own film in *Spider-Man: Homecoming* (2017), then both *Avengers: Infinity War* and *Avengers: Endgame*, followed by *Spider-Man: Far From Home* (2019). As one can see, the character appeared in ten films in the space of seventeen years, played by three different actors, with the Holland version in particular appearing in five films in the space of four years. While this frequency obviously delights fans who are eager to see their favorite superheroes on the screen as often as possible, it can also cause problems as rival studios become so eager to replicate the successes of the MCU that they rush films into production (see *Suicide Squad* [2016], *Justice League* [2017], and *Dark Phoenix* [2019]). This eagerness to capitalize on the genre's popularity was parodied in *Teen Titans Go! To the Movies* (2018) in its trailers for imaginary upcoming films like *Alfred the Movie*,[21] *Batmobile the Movie*, *Utility Belt the Movie*, and a Batman film that in its diegetic universe is appropriately called *Batman Again*.[22]

The superhero film is also worth studying for reasons not connected to industrial practices; one of the central assertions of this book is that the genre has been able to reflect the times in which it is made and the social, political, and ideological factors that shape them in palpable ways, a claim that has often been persuasively made about the products of national cinemas throughout the twentieth century. What might they have to say about the America of the new millennium which saw their construction? Is it a coincidence that the superhero renaissance emerges at almost the exact same period we refer to as the post-9/11 era? As many have argued there are striking similarities between the fears and anxieties dramatized in the modern superhero film and those of the United States in the first decades of the twenty-first century (see Kellner, 2009; Pheasant-Kelly, 2013). The question then might be what social function does the superhero film fulfill? Do they enable American (and indeed global) audiences to "escape from the very real horrors of international unrest and terrorism whose epic moment was September 11, 2001"?[23] We will see that what the genre as a whole reveals are a striking series of wish-fulfillment narratives which operate on both personal and cultural levels and a perfect example of André Bazin's assertion that popular American cinema has managed "in an extraordinarily competent way, to show American society just as it wanted to see itself."[24]

More than this, some have speculated that the cultural dominance of the superhero has affected the real world: that the emergence of Donald Trump might be blamed on the superhero film or that certain films from the genre are so important for audiences that *Black Panther* could be described as "a defining moment for Black America?"[25] As significant as these claims are, some go even further, suggesting that superheroes have emerged as god-like figures for twenty-first-century global cultures with books, articles, and editorials asking variations of the question Anne Billson posed in a *Telegraph* article: "Are Superheroes the New Gods?" (2013) in which she writes, "God is dead, but Superman lives!"[26] All of these ideas, each of which will be returned to in this book, are not suggestive of an ephemeral and disposable genre for children or one that should be patronizingly dismissed as "not cinema"; rather one which is rife with the paradoxes of the modern age and, above all, intimately connected to the cultures and times in which they are produced.[27]

This book is structured into five chapters, each exploring an aspect of the contemporary superhero film and each paired with two case studies illustrative of the chapter's central topic. The introduction will establish a variety of themes and a critical context that I will return to and build on to provide

Fig. 0.3 *The Dark Knight* (2008): How far does the superhero film mine the fears and anxieties of the times in which they are made, and should their protagonists be considered godlike figures in the new millennium?

a sense of continuity, development, and coherence throughout the book. Chapter 1, as one might expect, offers a framing of the parameters of the study. Should the superhero film be regarded as a genre in its own right? If so, what are its codes and conventions? What is its relationship to the comic books that formed it? For assistance we turn to Peter Coogan's indispensable study of the form *Superhero: The Secret Origin of a Genre* (2006), written just before what I have called the superhero renaissance had solidified. The opening case study takes on one of the most iconic heroes of the genre, Spider-Man, chosen especially because he is a character who helped define many of the codes and conventions discussed in both comic book and cinematic iterations. The second case study, the Deadpool series, provides a productive counterpoint to Spider-Man, as the character and the films he has featured in offer several challenges to these very same codes and conventions, but in intriguing ways adhere to them just as frequently.

Chapter 2 moves on to discuss the mythologies of the superhero genre by addressing how the heroic figures a culture produces have tended to embody the prevailing ideologies and values of the times in which they are formed and should be regarded not as simply crowd-pleasing tales but, in the case of superheroes, "the closest our modern culture has to myths."[28] This chapter turns to Richard Reynolds' *Superheroes: A Modern Mythology* (1992) to define the form from ideological perspectives, following such scholars as Jason Dittmer in *Captain America and the Nationalist Superhero: Metaphors, Narratives, and Geopolitics* (2012) and John Shelton Lawrence and Robert Jewett in *The Myth of the American Superhero* (2002). I consider the likes of Thor and Wonder Woman, who are *literally* gods, and Captain America, the Incredible Hulk, and the Watchmen, who are regarded as godlike figures within the diegetic worlds of their films. It is entirely logical then that we turn to perhaps two of the most culturally significant and enduring superheroes for this chapter's case studies: Superman and Batman. Both have been an indelible part of popular culture since their first appearances in comic book form at the end of the 1930s. A variety of writers have suggested that Superman is an embodiment of what many perceive as quintessential American values, yet the films in which he has featured from 1978 to the present day offer variations on this that show them to be closely connected to their respective cultural moments.[29] Batman remains the archetypal dysfunctional superhero in the cultural imaginary, providing an excellent contrasting figure in his many iterations: the Adam West era (1966–68); the two Burton films, *Batman* (1989) and *Batman Returns* (1992); the two Schumacher films, *Batman Forever* (1995), *Batman & Robin* (1997); the Christopher Nolan Dark Knight trilogy, comprised of *Batman Begins* (2005), *The Dark Knight* (2008), and *The Dark Knight Rises* (2012); and the incarnation of the character played by Ben Affleck in the DCEU in *Batman v Superman: Dawn of Justice* (2016), *Suicide Squad* (2016), and *Justice League* (2017), all of which were deconstructed in the witty and affectionate *The Lego Batman Movie* (2017).

After addressing the codes and conventions, and the mythologies of the superhero genre, chapters 3 and 4 are both concerned with what we might call the politics of representation. Carolyn Cocca, in *Superwomen: Gender, Power, and Representation* (2016) contended that

> while you do not have to have a perfect demographic match with a fictional character to identify with her or him, seeing someone who looks like you can have a positive impact on self-esteem. You are more likely to imagine yourself as a hero if you see yourself represented as a hero. Marginalized groups have been forced to "cross-identify" with those different to them while dominant groups have not. That is, because white males have been so overrepresented, women and people of color have had to identify with white

male protagonists. But white males have not had to identify with the small number of women and people of color protagonists.[30]

Cocca's observation here is not anecdotal but supported and confirmed by a variety of empirical studies conducted by a wide range of individuals and associations. With this in mind, chapter 3 examines how the superhero film has historically represented gender and sexuality on the screen. and whether accusations about it being a largely reactionary genre which has most often embodied conservative fantasies and has tended to marginalize superheroes who are not white, heterosexual, and male are as true in their contemporary incarnation as they might have been in previous eras. In terms of sexuality, I explore how the superhero film has been an emphatically heteronormative space with only rare and fleeting allusions to sexualities other than what is regarded as 'the norm' even though they are produced in an era and by a culture that is said to be more diverse than at any time in its history. The first case study for this section examines Wonder Woman, one of the rare superheroes to have been continuously published since her debut in *All Star Comics* no. 8 in October 1941. But despite being one of the most iconic of all superheroes she had never appeared in a live action film until she was featured as a supporting player in *Batman v Superman: Dawn of Justice* in 2016, in her own film, *Wonder Woman* (2017), and the sequel *Wonder Woman 1984* which followed in 2020. For the second case study I turn to the animated film series about a family of superheroes, in Pixar's *The Incredibles* (2004) and *Incredibles 2* (2018), both hugely impactful and successful on their release. I focus on aspects of the genre that are rarely highlighted: the domestic space and familial relations among superheroes. It might be argued that much had changed in the world and in the genre in the fourteen years between the two films, but rather than ignore these developments the sequel places changing attitudes toward gender roles in the new millennium at the center of its narrative.

Following on from this, Chapter 4 then interrogates the genre's portrayal of ethnicity with the acknowledgment that there have been very few superheroes who are not white as primary protagonists in superhero films. There have been African American characters in the genre, but the vast majority have been largely secondary (Falcon, War Machine, Cyborg, etc.), and the absence of Asian, Hispanic, and Arab superheroes or even characters is so pronounced that it becomes a problem even for the selection of case studies in this chapter as, at the time of writing, there are *absolutely none* of note that have been produced by American film companies and seen by general audiences. For the first case study we turn to the Will Smith vehicle *Hancock*, released in July 2008, the most successful superhero film with a black protagonist at the time of its release and a film that has been praised and criticized in almost equal measure. We then explore *Black Panther*, the eighteenth film in the Marvel Cinematic Universe, the first film with a black character as a protagonist in the series, and perhaps the most culturally impactful superhero film of the modern era.

In the book's final chapter, I look beyond the borders of the United States to consider superhero films made around the globe. What might they be able to say about the diverse cultures in which they are produced? How far do they deviate from the codes and conventions of the genre we established in chapter 1 and the mythologies explored in chapter 2? How are they similar to American films, which have a tremendous influence on them, and how do they differ? Moving between Spain, England, South Korea, the Philippines, Thailand, India, and other countries I examine whether foreign superhero films should be considered, as Anurima Chanda argues, not an example of "marginal cultural production" based on "mimicking"[31] but rather a process of cross pollination or transcreation, understood as "a transnational and translational instantiation of the superhero embedded in familial and vernacular conventions" of their own cultures.[32] The British superhero film *SuperBob* provides the book's penultimate case study and is a text that both engages with and deconstructs some of the essential tenets of the genre, which have been largely defined by American superhero films. It adopts what we might consider, with some qualification, particularly British elements into its narrative and style (characters, location, the mockumentary form, self-deprecating humor, etc.) while at the same time offering striking deviations from the codes and conventions of the genre. For the final case study, we turn to the phenomenal success of the Indian superhero series comprised of *Koi . . . Mil Gaya* (2003), *Krrish* (2006), and *Krrish 3* (2013). The films, directed by Rakesh Roshan and starring his son, Hrithik Roshan, have become one of the biggest franchises in Indian film history, expanding beyond the cinema to television, comics, and video games. As we habitually see with the American film industry, the films become bigger as the series progresses: with larger budgets, more

Fig. o.4 *Joker* (2019) became a cultural battleground on which a war of meaning was waged and was the first film from the genre to win an award as prestigious as the Golden Lion at Venice.

characters, increasing amounts of special effects, and more and more elaborate action sequences. The trilogy draws extensively and fairly explicitly on American superheroes like Spider-Man, Superman, and Batman; however, at the same time they are uniquely Indian and engage with their own cultural values and beliefs in never less than intriguing ways.

Just as defining a starting point for this reemergence of the superhero film has been challenging, even more so is speculation about when or even if it might end. Despite regular warnings that the genre had already reached a saturation point as early as 2014, this end does not seem to be coming any time soon, with 2018 and 2019 being remarkable successes for the genre.[33] Steven Spielberg, one of the central architects of blockbuster cinema in the four decades since the release of *Jaws* in 1975 commented that, like the Western before it, the superhero film could not go on indefinitely. He remarked:

> We were around when the Western died and there will be a time when the superhero movie goes the way of the Western. It doesn't mean there won't be another occasion where the Western comes back and the superhero movie someday returns. Of course, right

now the superhero movie is alive and thriving. . . . There will come a day when the mythological stories are supplanted by some other genre that possibly some young filmmaker is just thinking about discovering for all of us.[34]

Spielberg is of course correct in his assertion that genres fall in and out of favor with audiences, and there is no reason to assume that the superhero film will be any different. Indeed, some prominent voices, like that of James Cameron, who has done as much as Spielberg to define the contours of the Hollywood blockbuster, have even expressed a desire that it will, stating, "I'm hoping we'll start getting 'Avenger' fatigue here pretty soon."[35] The Western fell out of favor when audiences no longer found its narratives relevant and engaging, when the films no longer reflected the experiences and the values of the audiences that had once gone to see them en masse. The same fate will certainly befall the superhero film when it cannot tell the stories that people want to see in the ways they want to see them. But for now and for the foreseeable future we live in the age of the superhero, and the parameters of this genre, why it appeals to audiences across the globe, and what it has to say about the world we live in are the central questions this book seeks to explore.

1 THE CODES AND CONVENTIONS OF THE CONTEMPORARY SUPERHERO FILM

> Everybody loves a hero. People line up for them, cheer them, scream their names, and years later they'll tell how they stood in the rain for hours just to get a glimpse of the one who taught them to hold on a second longer. I believe there's a hero in all of us . . . that keeps us honest . . . gives us strength . . . makes us noble . . .
>
> —Aunt May in *Spider-Man 2*

> The superhero film can appear to be a genre in its own right, with identifiable tropes, conventions and iconography. These tropes include tragic loss, learning to use one's new powers, villains whose trajectory mirrors that of the hero, action sequences and conclusions that leave narrative points open for development in sequels to continue the franchise. However, the superhero film can also fit within the broader genres of the action film, science fiction, blockbuster, and the revenge narrative.
>
> —Vincent M. Gaine, "Genre and Superheroism: Batman in the New Millennium" (2011)

As Vincent M. Gaine observes, the superhero film is in a more complicated position with regards to genre than it initially appears. His assertion that it both *is* and *is not* a genre is certainly true, and there are scholars who have persuasively argued that it does fulfill all the functions of a genre and others who say that it does not. Central to this fluidity is one of its defining characteristics: its inherent malleability, as Henry Jenkins observes, it is a genre that "seems capable of absorbing and reworking all other genres."[1] Writing in 2008 before the release of *Iron Man* and the start of the MCU, Jenkins was still able to discern how the genre had begun to transform in the early years of the twenty-first century, and a cursory overview of the different types of superhero film provides an insight into this: from light-hearted and fantastical (*Fantastic Four* [2005], *Captain Barbell* [2003], *Max Steel* [2016]); comedic and parodic (*Kick Ass* [2010], *Guardians of the Galaxy* [2014], *Thor: Ragnarok* [2017]); family-oriented (*Shazaam* [2019], *Sky High* [2005], *Antboy* [2013]); horror-inflected (*The New Mutants* [2020], *Brightburn* [2019]); grounded and quasi-realistic (*Special* [2006], *Defendor* [2009]); quirky and offbeat (*Hellboy* [2004], *Deadpool* [2016]); centered on villains rather than heroes (*Suicide Squad* [2016], *Megamind* [2010], *Joker* [2019]); period set (*Wonder Woman* [2017], *Captain America: The First Avenger* [2010], *X-Men: First Class* [2011]); adult-oriented (*Watchmen* [2009], *Logan* [2017], *Bhavesh Joshi* [2018]); animated (*The Incredibles* [2004], *The Lego Batman Movie* [2017], *Spider-Man: Into the Spider-Verse* [2018]); part of the found-footage cycle (*Chronicle* [2012]) and those where we are asked to wonder whether what happens is real or inside the head of their protagonists (*Griff the Invisible* [2010], *Super* [2010], *Paper Man* [2009]). Even within the MCU as it continued one is able to clearly identify variations and efforts to revivify successive instalments in the franchise by appropriating stylistic and narrative devices from other genres: hence *Ant-Man* is very much a heist film as well as a superhero film; *Captain America: The Winter Soldier* (2014) is also a conspiracy thriller; and both *Spider-Man: Homecoming* and *Spider-Man: Far From Home* draw extensively from John Hughes's teen movies like *Sixteen Candles* (1984) and *The Breakfast Club* (1985).

The superhero film also proves interesting from the perspective of Robert Stam's often quoted taxonomy of genres in which he claims that "while some genres are based on story content (the war film), others are borrowed from literature (comedy, melodrama) or from other media (the musical). Some are performer-based (the Astaire-Rogers films) or budget-based (blockbusters), while others are based on artistic status (the art film), racial identity (Black cinema), location (the Western) or sexual orientation

(Queer cinema)."[2] At least two of these are relevant to the superhero film and perhaps even more: firstly "story content": as most superhero films feature a person or group of people who have some sort of ability that they might be born with or acquire in some way which enables them to commit acts which are regarded by many, although not all, as heroic. Secondly, literary borrowing: the genre could not exist without its continued connections to the rich history of the comic books where almost all of its iconic characters were created, in some cases—such as Batman, Superman, and Captain America—more than eighty years ago, during the so-called Golden Age of comic books from the 1930s to the 1950s. Others come from the Silver Age (mid-1950s to 1970s), such as the Fantastic Four (November 1961), the Incredible Hulk (May 1962), Iron Man (March 1963), Spider-Man (August 1963), and the X-Men (September 1963). Some are more recent creations, like the Watchmen (September 1986), Deadpool (February 1991), and Kick Ass (February 2008), or do not have their roots directly in comic books even though they are influenced by them, like the characters in *Hancock* and *The Incredibles*. However, whether comic books should be included in the category of "literature" or "other media" has been widely debated.[3]

Even taking into account their malleability, superhero films have a readily identifiable set of codes and conventions which a range of writers have explored for decades. It is the work of Peter Coogan, especially his *Superhero: The Secret Origin of a Genre* (2006), which proves the most valuable; his definitions are largely conceptual in nature, relating primarily to form and content rather than ideology, an aspect we will turn to in more detail in chapter 2. At the core of his analysis are the three categories of powers, identity, and mission that, he argues, have defined the genre since its beginning in comic books.[4] It is clear that Coogan has Superman in mind as a prototypical figure throughout his work, a fact entirely understandable given how iconic the character has been since his initial appearance in 1939. His shadow still loomed large in 2006, even though he had not appeared in film since 1987, and his reappearance was eagerly anticipated in the aptly titled *Superman Returns* in the same year. It is also noteworthy that Coogan's work was written on the eve of the renaissance this book is discussing, a few years before the genre found its "real voice" in 2008, according to Liam Burke. This provides us with a valuable perspective on how far modern incarnations of the genre might differ or not from those which preceded it.[5] Do the codes and conventions that he describes in 2006 still relate to the films made after? Or has the modern superhero film deviated from the comic book foundations on which it was built?

Powers

> But Dad always said our powers were nothing to be ashamed of, our powers made us special!
>
> —Dash in *The Incredibles* (2004)

It is the category of powers that Coogan understandably regards as "one of the most identifiable elements of the superhero genre"[6] and an aspect which distinguishes it from other varieties of science fiction and action films. Superheroes are, for the most part, in possession of some sort of power or ability that separates them from other heroic figures, although these powers come in a variety of guises: the superhero might be born with them (Wonder Woman, Hellboy, Krrish, Hancock, the Commander in *Sky High*, and Thor); given them by accident (Hulk, Spider-Man, the Flash, Cyborg, Cicak Man, Captain Barbell, SuperBob, and the ordinary teenagers Andrew, Matt, and Steve in *Chronicle*); choose to receive them (Captain America, Scarlet Witch, Black Panther); acquire them through extreme levels of training (Batman, Black Widow, Hawkeye); gain them through magical or religious circumstances (Shazam, Doctor Strange, Flying Jatt); construct or be given a suit or technological device which gives them powers (Iron Man, Cyborg, Bloodshot) or achieve power through combinations of these in the cases of characters like Wolverine, Blade, Spider-Man, and Deadpool. Some superheroes are more human than others, literally and figuratively, with no real powers or special abilities at all, but still identified as superheroes (Kick Ass, the Crimson Bolt in *Super*, Bhavesh and Sikander in *Bhavesh Joshi*).

The powers themselves can similarly be wide ranging: flight, super strength, invulnerability, super speed, telekinesis, invisibility, regenerative healing, with their usefulness and efficacy prompting debates between enthusiasts since the 1930s, as Freddy Freeman asks Billy Batson in *Shazam!*, "If you had one superpower what would you pick? Everybody chooses flight, you know why? *Because heroes fly!*" This debate is only slightly more popular than arguing who would win in a fight between superhero X and superhero Y? A question that, among other things, drew audiences to films like *Batman v Superman: Dawn of Justice* and *Captain America: Civil War*, which tended, on the whole, not to provide definitive answers, only questions for future sequels.[7]

Identity

> Who am I? You sure you wanna know?
> —Peter Parker/Spider-Man in *Spider-Man* (2002)

Coogan's concept of identity is still as inextricably tied to the genre as it has ever been with the personalities of superheroes frequently embodied in their choice of name and costume: from the unambiguous A adorned on Captain America's helmet and his red, white, and blue shield to the slightly more understated, although only just, lightning bolt emblazoned on the costume of the Flash to signify his amazing speed and the unassuming green poncho worn by David Dunn (Bruce Willis), otherwise known as the Overseer, in M. Night Shyamalan's Unbreakable trilogy (2000–2018), each character's name and costume are representative of not just their powers but also their attitude toward their superheroic status.[8] However, Coogan's suggestion that "the identity element comprises the codename and the costume, with the secret identity being a customary counterpart to the codename" is not quite as applicable to more recent superhero films as it was to those before the re-emergence of the genre.[9] Certainly, the costume is still key to a superhero's identity with even its transitions across decades being fundamental to how we are asked to understand any given character (witness the variations of Batman's costume changes from the spandex of the Adam West era). As the genre has become more familiar, characters within the films themselves provide a commentary on these costumes as a surrogate for audiences doing the same as Edna Mode did about the sartorial choices of superheroes in *The Incredibles* with her memorable "No capes!" rule, or when Wolverine (Hugh Jackman) on learning that a man able to shoot a red laser beam from his eyes is actually called Cyclops in *X-Men* turns to the wheelchair-bound Charles Xavier and asks "What do they call you . . . *Wheels*?"

It is in the arena of the secret identity that the genre has undergone a notable shift. Where it was once a central part of the superhero narrative in both comic books and films, the MCU has almost entirely erased this once fundamental trope, to the extent that very few of their superheroes have a secret identity and the usual narratives associated with them play little part in the series. In the comics Tony Stark kept his secret identity for decades, but in the cinematic world it is revealed at the end of the first film with his memorable "I am Iron Man," a line of dialogue that also ends *Iron Man 3* and are almost his last words before his death in *Avengers: Endgame*. In the DCEU the secret identity element is still present for characters such as Batman and Superman, but it is never a central part of the narrative in any meaningful way as it once was in earlier films featuring the characters.

Mission

> I can't lead a mission when the people I'm leading have missions of their own . . .
>
> —Steve Rogers/Captain America in
> *Captain America: The Winter Soldier*

The most discernible changes in Coogan's three categories come in those of "mission." In perhaps the most widely referred to section of his book he writes, "The superhero's mission is prosocial and selfless, which means that his fight against evil must fit in with the existing, professed mores of society and must not be intended to benefit or further his own agenda. The mission convention is essential to the superhero genre because someone who does not act selflessly to aid others in times of need is not heroic and therefore not a hero."[10] Films made before the modern era exemplify this concept almost without exception; across the four Superman films starring Christopher Reeve, Superman rarely questions what it really means to be the Man of Steel or if he should be Superman (except for a brief decision to retire for love in *Superman III*), and the same can be said for the first four films in the Batman franchise (1989–1997), where Batman/Bruce Wayne, whoever wears the cowl, never struggles with his identity, explicitly questions his mission, considers his mortality, or thinks about retiring in anything more than in a cursory fashion. Yet for the modern incarnations of both of these characters and for many other protagonists of the genre, these issues are placed at the center of their narratives: in Tony Stark's journey from hedonistic narcissist to self-sacrificing hero or Wolverine's reluctance to embrace his heroism from his initial appearance as a cage fighter in *X-Men* to his last in *Logan*, where he is buried somewhere on the Canadian border by his "daughter" Laura aka X-23. In the modern Batman films, both the Nolan and Snyder versions, Batman is defined by his crisis of identity about who or what he should be, even breaking his rule about killing in *Batman v Superman* in ways it is hard to imagine him doing in previous iterations through the 1980s and 1990s (although both Superman and Batman killed people fairly frequently in the early years of their comic books). In both these modern versions of the character *the cost* of being the Batman is one of their central motifs: Bale's Batman fakes his own death and retires in *The Dark Knight Rises*, and Affleck in *Batman v Superman* is an aging Batman driven to extremes by a desire for revenge on Superman after the events of *Man of Steel*. It is not that these characters do not ultimately embrace the "prosocial and selfless" mission that Coogan describes, but they wrestle with it and what it means in ways characters rarely if ever did before the genre returned to prominence in the 2000s. In a slightly more extended challenge to this, several more recent onscreen superheroes are decidedly antiheroes, with the best examples being Deadpool, explored as a case study later; the Punisher in the films *The Punisher* (2004) and *Punisher: War Zone* (2008); much of the cast of *Watchmen* (2009) and *Harley Quinn: Birds of Prey* (2020); and Hellboy, who featured in two idiosyncratic films by Guillermo del Toro: *Hellboy* (2004) and *Hellboy II: The Golden Army* (2006) before being rebooted by Neil Marshall in the poorly received *Hellboy* (2019). These characters embrace the superhero's mission to varying degrees, with most ultimately doing some kind of good if often by varying standards and complexities. The central point to observe here is that superheroes have become more vulnerable and human in modern superhero films and, at least superficially, more fallible, something audiences seem to have demanded from the genre as it has evolved. Whether this is sustained or meaningful is debatable, as it is something that is regularly criticized, as László Nemes, the director of *Son of Saul* (2015), did when he argued that superhero films are "unwatchable and false, boring and self-referential, a world of ideal people who don't behave as humans but more like machines."[11] But this does not seem to

Fig. 1.1 In *Iron Man* (2008) and films like it Peter Coogan's categories of "mission, identity, and powers" remain as central to the genre as they were in 1939, yet they have undergone revisions connected to the modern era.

correspond with either how the genre has changed in the modern era or the audience's experiences of it. When several fans were interviewed after *Avengers: Endgame* about the death or retirement of their favorite characters for an article by Kyle Kizu in *The Hollywood Reporter*, one remarked, "I think losing a friend is the best way to describe it." Another said, "It is like saying goodbye to someone you have grown up with and they can't hear you."[12] A young woman interviewed by Philadelphia television channel 6ABC Action News in a segment entitled "Philly Audiences Find Deeper Meaning in *Black Panther*" commented, "I'm just as excited about this movie as about when Barack Obama became the first African American president for the United States, I have that same exhilaration because I can hand down this to my grandchildren, they can see that it is possible for us to have black heroes."[13] Whether we agree with these fans or not, it is difficult to doubt the sincerity of their interactions with the superhero film, which suggests an affectual power and a complexity that critics of the genre are reluctant to acknowledge.

There are a number of other codes and conventions one can discern throughout the genre's lifespan, some formed prior to the renaissance we are exploring and some during it. Each is important to many but not all superhero films in this period, and sometimes they are deliberately and self-consciously challenged by certain films. Some of them are discussed in valuable books on the genre, such as Marc DiPaolo's *War, Politics and Superheroes: Ethics and Propaganda in Comics and Film* (2011); Liam Burke's *The Comic Book Film Adaptation: Exploring Modern Hollywood's Leading Genre* (2015); and Jeffrey Brown's *The Modern Superhero in Film and Television: Popular Genre and American Culture* (2016). These other conventions include:

1. The superhero often reaches maturity without having a relationship with his biological parents and has a tragic past that forms their identity as a superhero (Batman, Spider-Man, Iron Man, Superman, Superlópez, Shazam, etc.).

2. The superhero is opposed by a villain who often seems to be a shadow figure of the hero in terms of abilities and personality (Captain America and the Red Skull, Ant-Man and Yellow Jacket, Hulk and Abomination, Spider-Man and Venom, Iron Man and Whiplash/Obadiah Stane).

3. Justice and narrative resolution can only achieved through violent conflict.

4. The hero possesses a strict and often clearly defined moral code.

5. Prominent landmarks in the United States and all over the globe are destroyed.

6. Many films from the genre in the modern era make a conscious turn toward realism, which distances them from the fantastical excesses of earlier superhero films.

7. The superhero will be confronted by a dilemma, which Stephen Faller labeled as the "false dichotomy choice,"[14] in that they will be offered the seemingly impossible choice of saving either one party or another before ultimately saving both.

8. Civilians are rarely shown seriously injured or killed during the course of the film.

9. The films sometimes offer an insight into the alien, transhuman, or posthuman experience, whether that might be the "mutants" of the X-Men series, the "enhanced" of the MCU, the "metahumans" of the DCEU, or the "maanvars" of *Krrish 3*.[15]

10. The superhero is triumphant at the end of the narrative.

11. The superhero does not die at the film's climax.

Some of these elements are as prevalent in the genre as they have ever been; some have changed; and others are more emphatically a part of the modern superhero film than those made before the 2000s. Points 1–4 have been prominent in the superhero genre since the Golden Age comics and are still so central to the films that they are frequently commented on or parodied. The moral code talked of in (4) is now sometimes transgressed in ways it was not previously on the screen (see Superman killing Zod in *Man of Steel* and Batman's desire for revenge in *Batman v Superman*). With regards to (5) the development of CGI has made it possible to render destruction of landmarks and even entire cities photorealistically, with a remarkable detail and scale never possible before in the medium. Some have challenged the ethics of such wanton devastation being used for entertainment, labeling it "disaster porn" and connected it to the ubiquity of portable recording devices and the instantaneous transmission of live images of contemporary traumatic events such as 9/11, the Asian Tsunami (2004), and Hurricane Katrina (2005).[16] The producers of films from the superhero genre constantly seek ways to make it culturally relevant, for both artistic and commercial reasons; thus, they subsume current events, trends, and social discourse into its narratives. In the example of the disasters mentioned above this happens first unreflectively as in the destruction reveled in in *Man of Steel*; later, with more awareness, Tony Stark seeks to avoid it on the streets of Johannesburg in *Avengers: Age of Ultron*; then in *Captain America: Civil War* attempts to deconstruct it through the centralization of the Sokovia Accords while still continuing the practice, as does *Spider-Man: Far From Home* in the attacks on Venice and London, which are later revealed to be a plot by Mysterio in scenes that function as a commentary on the evolution of the genre itself. Aware that in the wake of the galaxy-wide destruction of *Avengers: Infinity War* people need more to move them, Mysterio tells the special effects team who create his illusions, "You know what? Double the damage—*more casualties, more coverage!*"

Category (6) concerns itself with what I have elsewhere referred to as the "veristic turn" that the genre embraced in the more recent period.[17] The assertion here is not that superhero texts are realistic in the usual definition of the term but that they are *grounded* in reality to a much greater extent than the superhero films made before. The diegetic worlds where the majority of modern superheroes reside are quite distinct from the fantasies of the Donner-era Superman films or the Burton or Schumacher Batman films. This turn toward "reality" is not unprecedented in American genre cinema; as Leo Braudy has observed, many stagnant genres over the years have become revivified with an "injection, usually of 'realism.' " Grant Morrison, the award-winning comic book writer, observed this change and stated: "With no way to control the growing unreality of the wider world, writers and artists attempted to tame it in fictions that became more and more 'grounded,' down-to-earth, and rooted in the self-consciously plausible."[18] The results of this turn are a stylistic realism afforded by advances in CGI and a humanization of the characters in most films from the genre. This can be observed narratively, stylistically, and also in the characterization of both heroes and villains: witness the difference between Jack Nicholson's portrayal of the Joker and that by Heath Ledger and Joaquin Phoenix, or Terence Stamp's Zod and Michael Shannon's.

Points 7–11 have all been integral to the genre for decades but have undergone significant changes in recent years. In (7) Faller's "false dichotomy choice" is still most often adhered to but is sometimes transgressed, for example, in Batman's failure to save Rachel in *The Dark Knight* or Spider-Man's failure to save Gwen Stacey in *The Amazing Spider-Man 2*, both of which result in their deaths. This is connected to (8), which again is rarely contravened with civilians hardly ever dying, though sometimes they are permitted to do so if it is offscreen (see *Wonder Woman*) or we are informed about it in subsequent films and not at that moment (see *Captain America: Civil War*). A rare challenge to this comes in *Logan*, where the Munson family, who offer Wolverine and Professor X shelter in their farmhouse, are brutally killed onscreen, even the young boy, Nate Munson.

The two final categories are connected to each other; rarely do superheroes not emerge victorious at the climax of their film and rarely do they die. In the modern era this has been challenged somewhat: did Helmet Zemo achieve his goal of getting the superheroes to fight one another in *Captain America: Civil War*? Did Loki win in *Thor: Dark World* when he tricked his brother into thinking he was dead and assumed the throne of Asgard? Did Surtur win in *Thor: Ragnarok* when he destroyed Asgard? No film did this as emphatically as *Avengers: Infinity War*, where at the climax the superheroes fail to prevent Thanos causing the "snap" and erasing from existence half of all living beings throughout the galaxy.

Yet audiences surely knew that somehow everything would be restored a year later in *Avengers: Endgame* even if they did not know how . . . which indeed it was. On the matter of superheroes dying, some minor characters have been allowed to (Quicksilver, Angel Salvadore, Darwin, Yondu), and other, more important heroes have died only for their deaths to later be revealed as illusions (Loki, Nick Fury, Batman) or impermanent (Superman, the victims of the snap). Once again it is *Avengers: Infinity War* and its sequel, *Avengers: Endgame*, that offer the most comprehensive challenges to this, something the creators of the franchise perhaps felt they had earned with the preceding films in the series, killing off Heimdall, Vision, Loki, Gamora, and Black Widow, although of these only the death of Heimdall appeared permanent as Marvel announced that the others would appear in upcoming films or television shows shortly after. Most notably, *Avengers: Endgame* saw the death of the character that had started it all in 2008, Tony Stark, with Iron Man bowing out of the franchise after eleven years while sacrificing himself to save the world. In Stark's case it was not an example of the false sacrifice that is so common in the genre, in which the hero seems to have given their life but miraculously survives, but a genuine one and all the more potent for it.[19]

Fig. 1.2 Are we to consider *Brightburn* (2019) a superhero film or a reaction to the now familiar codes and conventions of the genre?

Case Study: Spider-Man

> With great power comes great responsibility. This is my gift, my
> curse. Who am I? I'm Spider-Man.
> —Peter Parker/Spider-Man in *Spider-Man* (2002)

> [Spider-Man is] part of our collective consciousness . . . (and) would
> probably be recognized anywhere in the world regardless of differ-
> ences in race, language, creed, or any other grouping, and whether
> or not the individuals had read a story, seen or movie, watched a
> television programme or played a video game related to him.
> —Robert G. Weiner, "Sequential Art and Reality" (2009)

Perhaps the most famous superhero of all alongside Superman and
Batman, the character of Spider-Man appeared for the first time in comic
book form in *Amazing Fantasy* no. 15 (August 1962) but not in a major
feature film until 2002. Such has been the impact of Spider-Man that
one might argue that he is one of the rare superheroes to transcend the
medium, becoming as famous as a brand as he is a character, found on
duvets, lunch boxes, and pajamas, as well as in cartoons and video games.
There seems to be a general consensus among scholars and fans that one
of the primary reasons for Spider-Man's popularity is his *relatability*, that
of the vast number of superheroes he is the one most like those that have
historically populated the core demographic of the genre whether in its
literary or cinematic domains.[20] As Miles Morales says in the final lines of
Spider-Man: Into the Spider-Verse, "*Anyone* can be Spider-Man. *You* could
wear the mask. If you didn't know that before, I hope *you* know it now."

In most iterations Spider-Man is the high school student Peter Parker,
a smart but not very popular teenager; most importantly, he is quite ordinary.
When he is bitten by a radioactive spider on a school trip Peter is granted
superpowers of the arachnidan variety which include enhanced strength,
agility and the ability to climb walls. As Lisa Purse writes in *Contemporary
Action Cinema* (2011), even the way he gets his abilities is connected to how
normal Peter is, and the "gaining and discovery of powers plays here [in
Spider-Man] like the typical growing pains and discomforts of puberty."[21]
Raimi's 2002 film and the two films which followed it in his trilogy, *Spider-
Man 2* (2004) and *Spider-Man 3* (2007), established some of the defining

Fig. 1.3 "He's just a kid": power, responsibility, and vulnerability in *Spider-Man* (2002).

tropes of the new forms of the genre that we observed in chapter 1 and also provide a vivid illustration of Reynolds's categories of powers, identity, and mission. When Peter initially seeks to profit from the powers he has been accidentally given it results in the death of his uncle Ben, which forces him to come to terms with the weight of responsibility they come with. It is not a coincidence that *Spider-Man* opens with the question used as an epigraph for this case study, "Who am I?" and ultimately concludes with an answer at the end of the film: "With great power comes great responsibility. This is my gift, my curse. Who am I? I'm Spider-Man," six words which framed the role of the superhero throughout the decade and beyond.

Raimi's film was shot before, during, and after the terrorist attacks on New York in September 2001 and emphasizes the humanity and at times the vulnerability of Maguire's Peter Parker/Spider-Man in ways which would echo through the genre in the subsequent years, with its scenes of New Yorkers coming together in a spirit of unity read by many as deliberate allusions to the aftermath of 9/11.[22] The two subsequent films by Raimi followed the pattern we can often observe in modern sequels in the blockbuster age: expanded production budgets (from $139 to $200 to $258 million), dramatically larger cast of characters, more extensive use of special effects and even greater levels of action and spectacle. The second film of the trilogy is widely regarded as a benchmark of the modern superhero film genre, where action sequences provide both the kinaesthetic spectacle that audiences demand and character development in memorable scenes like Doctor Octopus's (Alfred Molina) bank robbery and the subsequent battle on a New York subway train that culminates in New Yorkers shielding a wounded Peter Parker from harm. The third film in the trilogy is less fondly remembered, justifiably so, as its messy and chaotic narrative provides ample evidence of what transpires when films move into production in order to meet a release date, a too common occurrence in the modern era. Yet it does provide Maguire's Peter Parker with a conclusion to his tenure as the character in ways that Andrew Garfield never had as plans for a third film after his *Amazing Spider-Man* and *Amazing Spider-Man 2* were abruptly canceled. Even though they made $757 and $708 million worldwide, the bar for what constitutes financial success for such top-tier characters had been raised to the extent that they were considered to have underwhelmed at the box office. Perhaps sensing this Jon Watts's *Spider-Man: Homecoming* jettisons the canonical origin story and the figure of Uncle Ben, locating the film much more in high school than any of the previous versions with Tom Holland, a teenager, playing Spider-Man rather than someone in their mid-twenties (Tobey Maguire) or even their thirties (Andrew Garfield). *Spider-Man: Homecoming* is about Peter attempting to reconcile himself with his powers, identity, and mission while trying to be a normal teen. All through the film he is driven to prove himself as a mature adult, and it is only at the climax, when he is finally offered the chance to actually become an Avenger, that he changes his mind and declines, preferring to stay "just" a high school kid for the last few years that he is able to. Peter's journey continued in *Spider-Man: Far From Home*, set in a post-snap *and* post-blip world in the aftermath of Tony Stark's death in *Avengers: Endgame*, a film released just a few months before, where Peter is forced to come to terms with the absence of his mentor while those living in the diegetic world of the MCU wonder who will take Iron Man's place. Peter meets the seemingly heroic Quentin Beck, a.k.a. Mysterio, who is later revealed to be a disgruntled former employee of Tony Stark seeking to position himself as Iron Man's heir apparent, even self-consciously designing his costume to appeal to as broad a demographic as possible, understanding as Richard Reynolds does how important the costume is to a superhero's identity; as the high schooler Brad observes,

Fig. 1.4 Recast, rebranded, rebooted, and resuited: *Spider-Man: Homecoming* (2017).

"He's like Iron Man *and* Thor rolled into one!" Keenly aware of its position as the twenty-third film in the MCU and bringing phase 3 to an end, the film concludes with one of the most memorable cliffhangers in the franchise's history as Quentin Beck reveals Spider-Man's true identity to the whole world.[23] Given the frequency of Spider-Man's appearances in the MCU until then (five films in four years), fans might have thought they would not have to wait too long to find out what happened next, but contract disputes between rival studios Disney and Sony placed the character in more jeopardy, for a few weeks at least, than his diegetic antagonists like Green Goblin and the Vulture had ever been able to.

Just as importantly, the cinematic universe of Spider-Man continued to develop in 2018 with the release of the animated *Spider-Man: Into the Spider-Verse*, which won an Academy Award for Best Animated Film. Rather than a mere side project as it might initially have appeared to be, the film updated and reconfigured Spider-Man lore, reinvigorating the character as much as if not more than his integration into the MCU has done. The film presents Spider-Man across a myriad of dimensions, commenting on reboot culture in the process by featuring not only Peter Parker but also Miles Morales, Spider-Man Noir, Peni Parker, and even Spider-Ham. Miles Morales, a multi-racial schoolboy, is at the center of the film in a narrative which affectionately deconstructs many of the tropes of the genre at a time when some had become jaded with repetitions of the formula.

Case Study: Deadpool

> I may be super, but I'm no hero. . . .
> —Deadpool in *Deadpool* (2016)

> As he kills his enemies with both gruesomeness and glee (all while telling us about it directly), we soon learn that Deadpool doesn't adhere to the same code of ethics guiding such upstanding super-heroes such as Superman and Captain America.
> —Blair Davis, *Comic Book Movies* (2018)

For our second case study we turn to a much more recent addition to the canon of superheroes, Rob Liefeld and Fabian Nicieza's Deadpool, a character who made his first appearance on the page in *The New Mutants* no. 98 (February 1991). As often as people have suggested that Spider-Man and the films that have featured him should be regarded as emblematic of the codes and conventions which have defined the superhero genre, just as many have suggested Deadpool deconstructs them.[24] In the comics the character initially appeared as a villain but soon evolved into the antihero that he is now widely known and appears in the film series as, played by the charismatic Canadian actor Ryan Reynolds. In both versions Deadpool (Wade Wilson) is a mercenary with regenerative powers that make him seemingly impossible to kill, who wields dual katanas and is characterized by his acerbic sense of humor and his tendency to break the fourth wall as, unlike most characters in the genre, he is entirely aware that he is fictional. In the comics this most frequently occurs with direct addresses to the reader, as in the cover of *Deadpool* no. 43 where he calls out, "Hey you there, buying this book!! Can you call me a taxi?" or acknowledging the fact that he knows he is in the comic book you are reading, as in *Deadpool* no. 28, when Bullseye asks him, "How long has it been?" and he replies, "Issue sixteen, Greece," or in even more challenging ways as in *Deadpool Team-Up* no. 885 he says, "No, I got it. If this is a comic book I can just dig back a few pages and warn myself to keep Hellcow out of the sun" as he cuts through the pages, returning to an earlier part of the story to outwit

Fig. 1.5 "A fourth wall break inside a fourth wall break? That's like, sixteen walls!"
Ryan Reynolds in *Deadpool* (2016).

the antagonist. In film Deadpool also originally briefly appeared as a villain in the disappointing *X-Men Origins: Wolverine* (2009), where he was also played by Ryan Reynolds. Somehow the actor was able to return to the character five years later in a film written by Rhett Reese and Paul Wernick and directed by Tim Miller. Studio executives at Fox must have been concerned how the superhero's irreverent and adult-oriented sensibilities would translate to a profitable film in a marketplace full of family-friendly superhero adventures, but after test footage was leaked in July 2014 and received extremely positively, the film was green-lit with a modest budget, by genre standards, of $58 million, the same year as *Captain America: Civil War* (2016) and *Batman v Superman: Dawn of Justice* (2016) both cost $250 million to produce, and *Suicide Squad* (2016) $175 million. These four films ended up in the top ten domestic box office earners of the year, with *Deadpool* earning a remarkable $783 million worldwide, making it, at the time of its release, the second most successful R-rated film ever, after *Passion of the Christ* (2004), a feat that even Deadpool himself commented upon in *Deadpool 2* with the line "I'm in the same sentence as Jesus . . . *Passion of the Christ* then me."

The film follows Wade Wilson, a former Special Forces soldier who contracts cancer and undergoes a mysterious and painful experimental cure orchestrated by the immoral scientist Francis Freeman, otherwise known as Ajax (Ed Skrein). Wade's cancer is cured, and he is also given superhuman strength, regenerative powers, and enhanced reflexes, but the process leaves him permanently disfigured and possessing a face that, as his friend Weasel suggests, "looks like an avocado had sex with an older, more disgusting avocado." The film and its sequel successfully adapt the signature metatextual devices of the comics by having Wade continually break the fourth wall and speak directly to the audience or having diegetic characters refer to the plot, a process that begins as early as the film's opening credits, which refer to the cast as "hot chick" and "British villain" in a story written by "the real heroes here" and directed by an "overpaid tool." Such techniques are not necessarily a distancing device, as they are commonly regarded as; Tom Brown's *Breaking the Fourth Wall* argues that they might in actual fact "enrich our appreciation of the fiction and the characters,"[25] something especially relevant to the superhero genre given how far audiences are now immersed in the codes and conventions we explored at the start of this chapter.[26]

The film acknowledges on multiple occasions that the Deadpool character they are watching is played by the actor Ryan Reynolds, who at that time had already starred in numerous superhero films, such as *Blade: Trinity* (2004), *Green Lantern* (2011), and *X-Men Origins: Wolverine*, and as the imaginary Captain Excellent in the small independent film *Paper Man* (2009). He sometimes offers explicit criticisms of his previous roles as in when Wade Wilson pleads with the scientists, "Please don't make the super-suit green! *Or animated!*" The references come at such a pace that it is hard to keep track of them, and this seems specifically designed to prompt audiences to return to the film multiple times in the cinema and later at home. The first film references a diverse range of texts from *127 Hours* (2010) to *Cobra* (1986), and *The Golden Girls* (NBC, 1985–1992) to *American Beauty* (1999) and Judy Blume's novel *Are You There God? It's Me, Margaret* (1970). The sequel is just as broad, encompassing the likes of *Say Anything* (1989), *Basic Instinct* (1992), and *Yentl* (1983). As Deadpool's face is covered for the majority of the film the writers are able to change or substitute dialogue, adding contemporary references in ways most live-action films are not able to do. The cowriter Paul Wernick stated "We've said it before; we can put words into his mouth up until the very last moment, so we're writing this movie until it locks—two, three weeks before it comes out."[27]

The most frequent allusions are to Deadpool's place in the genre, his status as a superhero, and in particular his relationship to the X-Men universe (2000-), which by the time of the release of *Deadpool* had lasted for sixteen years and featured seven films. At the time of his first film Deadpool was very much a minor character in the franchise, a fact he comments on in the opening lines to the audience: "Oh, hello! I know, right? Whose balls did I have to fondle to get my own movie?" Later, walking around Xavier's Academy for Gifted Youngsters from the X-Men films, a place he calls "Neverland mansion" and remarks that it "blows up every few years," Deadpool wonders why there are only two X-Men there and little known ones at that, Colossus and Negasonic Teenage Warhead, suggesting, "It's almost like the studio couldn't afford another X-Man." Yet by the time of the sequel *Deadpool 2* the character had become *the* star of the franchise, and the joke is replayed, with this time Deadpool remarking, "You think the studio would throw us a bone; they can't just dust off one of the famous X-Men?" as he walks past a room which contains Cyclops, Beast, Professor X, Storm, Night Crawler, and Quicksilver, all played by the same actors who have portrayed them in the recent films that started with *X-Men: First Class*.

After the incredible and unexpected success of the first film, the sequel expanded upon it in a number of ways, not just with its bigger budget of $110 million but also by further pursuing these metatextual references and in-jokes to the extent that it was even rereleased in December of the same year in two other versions. The first, a slightly more family-friendly edition known as *Once Upon a Deadpool*, featuring a framing device that had Fred Savage reprising his role as "the Grandson" from *The Princess Bride* (1987) and the second, *Deadpool: The Super Duper Cut* (2018), an even more violent and profane extended cut of the film with fifteen extra minutes of action.[28] All three versions of the sequel continue Deadpool's adventures after the death of his partner, Vanessa (Morena Baccarin), and the arrival of a mysterious cyborg from the future, Cable (Josh Brolin), who is determined to kill a child who he believes will grow up to be a serial killer. It becomes more irreverent and audacious, if slightly less engaging than the first film, even featuring unannounced, hard-to-spot cameos by two of the biggest movie stars in the world, Brad Pitt and Matt Damon. Cable becomes the primary target of the film's metatextual jokes; with Deadpool calling him "a grumpy old fucker with a Winter Soldier arm" then asking him, "You're so dark, are you sure you're not from the DC universe?" Finally telling the character to "Zip it Thanos!" referring to the fact that the actor Josh Brolin also played the villain of *Avengers: Infinity War*, released in that same summer. The film's most brazen challenge to

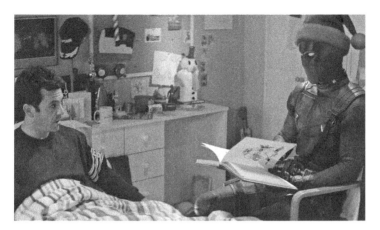

Fig. 1.6 *Once Upon a Deadpool* (2018) mischievously appropriates the frame story from *The Princess Bride* (1987).

audience expectations is the time it spends building up characters known as the X-Force, who had first appeared in *New Mutants* no. 100 (April 1991) like Domino, Bedlam, Shatterstar, Zeitgeist, Vanished, and the rather ordinary Peter (Rob Delaney), a team that Deadpool calls "tough, morally flexible, and young enough so they can carry this franchise for the next ten to twelve years," and even going so far as to feature them prominently in the advertising for the film, leading audiences to speculate that they might also be a part of a potential X-Force spin off movie . . . only to kill them off one by one, except for Peter.

2 THE MYTHOLOGIES OF THE CONTEMPORARY SUPERHERO FILM

People need dramatic examples to shake them out of apathy, and I can't do that as Bruce Wayne. As a man, I'm flesh and blood. I can be ignored. I can be destroyed. But as a symbol, as a symbol I can be incorruptible, I can be everlasting. . . .

—Bruce Wayne in *Batman Begins* (2005)

Every Hollywood film and television narrative, though created for reasons of entertainment and profit (and sometimes art), is in fact a cultural artefact; a representation of the values, mythos, ideologies and assumption of the culture that produced it . . . these narratives shape our collective consciousness, affirming accepted ideological and cultural beliefs/mythos and, sometimes, modifying them.

—Robert Cotter (2013)

The mythology that this chapter refers to is the process by which any given culture, from the modern era to antiquity, creates its own characters and tales which both dramatize and perpetuate the culture's prevailing values and ideals. Thus it is a mythology which belongs to a rich cultural tradition of storytelling but also one in the Barthesian sense as a participatory cultural discourse the likes of which Richard Slotkin called "a complex of narratives that dramatizes the world vision and historical sense of a people or culture, reducing centuries of experience into a constellation of compelling metaphors . . . [which] provides a scenario or prescription for action, defining and limiting the possibilities for human response to the universe."[1] As many have articulated, one can tell a great deal about a culture by the narratives that it produces and the heroes which feature in them. Just as the Vikings had tales of Odin, Thor, Freya, SkaÐi, and Loki; the English have looked to Robin Hood, Saint George, King Arthur and his knights; and late nineteenth-century America turned to mythologised stories of Wyatt Earp, Davy Crockett, and Jesse James. In the twentieth century and into twenty-first, contemporary Western culture has found its heroic ideals embodied in comic book heroes like Superman, Batman, Captain America, and Spider-Man.

Of course, these characters are first and foremost designed to entertain and, in the modern era, sell cinema tickets, copies of films on DVD and Blu-ray, and licenses to digital devices, but at the same time they fulfill a very particular social role in how they reify and perpetuate cultural norms, values, and behavioral patterns in ways not always intended by those who create them. If the characters deviate too far from the desires of audiences or do not adhere to this social contract, the result might well be a failure to resonate; as Asa Berger writes, "There is a fairly close relationship, generally, between a society and its heroes; if a hero does not espouse values that are meaningful to his readers, there seems little likelihood that he will be popular."[2]

Key to this popularity and indeed one of the primary pleasures derived from the superhero—whether it might be tales of Batman from the United States, Odysseus from Greek mythology, Iktomi of the Lakota, Chử Đồng Tử of the Vietnamese, or Captain Barbell of the Philippines—is how it embodies a range of wish-fulfillment fantasies at both personal and cultural levels. As Will Brooker maintains, "Superheroes are about wish-fulfilment. They're about imagining a better world and creating an alternate vision of yourself—bigger, brighter, bolder, than the real thing—to patrol and protect it. That's the way it has always been, right from the start."[3] However, what this "better world" might be and what its implications are should be considered inherently ideological in a range of ways. As individuals we project ourselves onto the screen through identification with these figures, thrilling to their powerful individual fantasies about who we could be: stronger, faster, smarter, more virile, and more attractive. This particular idea might be

Fig. 2.1 The wish-fulfilment fantasies of the superhero genre at their most explicit in *Shazam!* (2019).

considered as more relevant to the superhero film than to other genres as it is something encoded within it, literalized on the screen as many of its heroes begin ordinary, like us, and undergo a fundamental change in ways we might dream of repeating ourselves: the teenager Peter Parker, bitten by a radioactive spider on a school trip, which results in his becoming a famous superhero; Peter Quill in *Guardians of the Galaxy*, an "ordinary" boy from Missouri who becomes the savior of the world; the puny Steve Rogers, who is transformed through an experimental government secret program into the iconic Captain America; or William "Billy" Batson, an orphan chosen to be the "Champion of Eternity" by an ancient wizard called Shazam. These characters already possess something within themselves that is brought to the fore by the superheroic powers they are given, a trope that reflects of our own desire and belief that *we are special too*.

But more than this, many of these characters, who are, not coincidentally, all American, function as representatives of broader cultural and social values connected to the society and culture that formed them. In this sense they are embodiments of what John Shelton Lawrence and Robert Jewett call the "American Monomyth" in their book of the same name (1977). In their later book, *The Myth of the American Hero* (2002), they maintain that American incarnations of heroic narratives depart from Joseph Campbell's accounts of common mythological tropes in his iconic *Hero with a Thousand Faces* (1949) as they focus not on initiation but redemption. They argue that:

> The monomythic hero claims surpassing concern for the health of the community, but he never practices citizenship. He unites a consuming love of impartial justice with a mission of personal vengeance that eliminates due process of law. He offers a form of leadership without paying the price of political relationships or responding to preferences of the majority. In denying the ambivalence and complexity of real life, where the moral landscape offers choices in various shades of gray rather than in black and white, where ordinary people muddle through life and learn to live with the many poor choices they have made, and where the heroes that do exist have feet of clay, the monomyth pictures a world in which no humans really live. It gives Americans a fantasy land without ambiguities to cloud the moral vision, where the evil empire of enemies is readily discernible, and where they can vicariously (through identification with the superhero) smite evil before it overtakes them.[4]

These connections to the culture that created them lead many to conclude that superhero stories have some sort of propagandistic function, as Jason Dittmer does in his book *Captain America and the Nationalist Superhero: Metaphors, Narratives, and Geopolitics* (2012), where he refers to characters like Captain America and Superman as nationalist superheroes. Dittmer and other authors like Dan Hassler-Forrest argue that contemporary superheroes should be considered the preeminent embodiments of the neoliberal age, representatives and indeed perpetuators of the economic, political, and cultural system that is characterized by "sweeping privatization, the financialization of the economy, the rise of technocracy over democracy, and the normalization of itself as the only possible system of organizing society."[5] They are indeed manifestations of the desire for simple solutions to the complicated problems of our era, authoritarian figures framed in such a way that for many audience members they are apolitical—much as neoliberalism has, as George

Monbiot contends, become so pervasive "that we seldom even recognise it as an ideology."[6] Yet the choices of what stories a culture tells to itself are inherently political, and many of the genre's most famous characters contribute to "the idea that the United States is not just the richest and most powerful of the world's more than two hundred states but also the most politically and morally exceptional."[7] If the majority of the world's superheroes come from the United States, must that not mean the United States itself is extraordinary? The most pertinent example of this in recent years is Iron Man and the many MCU films he featured in, which, Tanner Mirrlees convincingly argues, reinforces three separate but interconnected aspects of American power: "US economic power (as a Hollywood blockbuster and synergistic franchise), US military power (as a DOD-Hollywood co-produced militainment) and cultural power (as a national and global relay for US imperial ideologies)."[8]

Mirrlees is certainly correct, but the modern superhero has found this a more difficult process to navigate than previous iterations of the genre, which were unabashed in their embrace of patriotism: witness the transition of Superman and his once defining phrase of "truth, justice, and the American way," a line of dialogue that was synonymous with the character for decades but has been erased from recent films. Superman's connections to the state in the Reeve era are fairly unambiguous (interactions with the U.S. president, American military and repeated visits to the Whitehouse), but after a twenty year hiatus from the cinema the character presented some challenges on his return in the aptly titled *Superman Returns* and then *Man of Steel*, where "truth, justice, and the American way" had markedly different associations for much of the world in the wake of the War on Terror. Thus, the majority of new superhero films featuring iconic characters attempt to mediate the jingoism of previous eras, resulting in the modern-Superman being presented quite palpably as simultaneously a global citizen as well as an American in order not to alienate international audiences in an age where global box office receipts are more important than ever. Similarly, the Iron Man films portray a traumatized and conflicted Tony Stark who rejects the military-industrial complex and the government while at the same continuing to produce high-tech weapons of destruction and vanquishing America's enemies at home and abroad. It must have been a difficult task for Kevin Feige and director Joe Johnston to bring Captain America into the modern era, a character famous for being quite literally formed by the state (even though the comics have been exploring this for decades) and about whom his cocreator Joe Simon said, "He was a modern day Uncle Sam."[9] Correspondingly his contemporary iteration is more ambiguous and, at least on the surface, offers some partial challenges to the nationalism historically associated with the character. This was achieved by setting the first film *Captain America: The First Avenger*, during the Second World War, free from the complexities of the post-9/11 era. When he was brought into the present the threats he faced were primarily apocalyptic in *The Avengers* and its sequels, *Age of Ultron*, *Infinity War*, and *Endgame*. The only ambiguity emerges in the crisis of identity the character undergoes in *Winter Soldier*—with its very contemporary explorations of surveillance culture and governmental duplicity through fairly explicit evocations of the ethics of preemptive strikes and the USA PATRIOT Act—and the ethical dilemma at the heart of *Captain America: Civil War*. Both films are only superficially critical of the cultures that produce them; instead, they suggest that America is more than its institutions and that it is its core values and principles, embodied in Cap, which make America great and distinguishes it from every other country in the world.

It is for many of the reasons articulated above that the superhero film is justifiably regarded as a conservative and largely reactionary genre, offering solutions that are exclusively undemocratic and violent, a "mythic massage" that "soothes and satisfies. It imparts the relaxing feeling that society can actually be redeemed by anti-democratic means."[10] If many of these ideas about the superhero film here sound familiar it is because the genre should be considered a direct descendent of the Western. While far removed on the surface they share essential DNA in terms of their social significance, their narratives, and their ideological patterns. In both, "real men" are strong, self-reliant, courageous, and resolute; simplistically drawn bad guys are there to be vanquished; women are to be revered and saved and adored; the law is inherently unreliable; and the only answer to a problem, regardless of what it might be, is righteous and redemptive violence.[11] The superhero and films that contain him (as they are most definitely primarily about men) have largely replaced the Western hero in the cultural imaginary and perform a similar cultural function. Instead of being raised on Western serials screened almost perpetually on television and playing "Cowboys and Indians" in the backyard, today's young people, the Superhero Generation, are raised on superhero narratives and play with (and as) Iron Man, Superman, Batman, Captain America, and Spider-Man. James Mangold's *Logan* is perhaps the most explicit example of this, with its direct evocations of *Shane* (1953), *The Cowboys* (1972), and *Unforgiven* (1992), but it can be found in many entrants to the superhero genre. *Logan* is set on the border between Texas and Mexico and casts an older, jaded Wolverine as an outcast, reluctant to look after a young Mexican orphan girl who he discovers not only has powers similar to his but also is his "daughter." Mangold draws from the rich history of the Western, revivifying the superhero film in the process. He stated, "We're making kind of a Western. . . . For me, the key is not to think about making a comic-book movie but to think about making a movie and just let the fact that your characters are superheroes be a reality."[12] The film was widely received

Fig. 2.2 The superhero/western hybrid that is *Logan* (2017) both deconstructs and contributes to the mythology of the genre.

as such, with Joshua Rivera observing in the title of his review of the film in *GQ*, "Finally, Wolverine as Old John Wayne."[13]

Colin McArthur argued in 1972 that genres should be considered a dialogue between films and the cultural moment in which they are made, theorizing that "the western and the gangster film have a special relationship with American society. Both deal with critical phases of American history. It could be said that they represent America talking to itself about, in the case of the western, its agrarian past, and in the case of the gangster film/thriller its urban technological present."[14] If this is indeed the case, then it is reasonable to speculate about what the rebirth of the superhero film says about American society in the new millennium. Is it a reconsolidation of America's global role after 9/11 and during the War on Terror? One which occurred in the real world and was refought and replayed on the cinema screens in films shown all over the globe in an era which presented a significant challenge to American conceptions of itself? Lisa Purse argues that "it is likely that the ongoing popularity of the superhero film throughout the 2000s represents a desire amongst audiences to explore heroism and its motivations in a context safely divorced from the ethical dilemmas and complications of real-world politics and war in Iraq and Afghanistan"[15] alleging that they provide a safe environment for some issues to explored, but she is only partially correct; superhero films do immerse themselves in contemporaneous debates in ways the genre had previously shied from, if only ever in highly mediated forms. Thus *Iron Man* opens in Afghanistan and is about an arms dealer turned hero in the midst of the War on Terror era; *Black Panther* concerns itself with issues at the very heart of the African American community in 2018; and *Captain Marvel* explores aspects of gender identity in the wake of #MeToo (October 2017) and Time's Up (January 2018), with each of these films embodying the limitations and potentialities of the genre in never less than interesting ways.

Case Study: Superman

> All this time I've been living my life the way my father saw it. Righting wrongs for a ghost, thinking I'm here to do good. Superman was never real. Just the dream of a farmer from Kansas . . .
> —Superman in *Man of Steel* (2013)

Each of these heroes is gifted with such powers that he could actually take over the government, defeat the army, or alter the equilib-
rium of planetary politics. On the other hand, it is clear that each of
these characters is profoundly kind, moral, faithful to human and
natural laws, and therefore it is right (and it is nice) that he use his
powers only to the end of good. In this sense the pedagogic message of these stories would be, at least on the plane of children's
literature, highly acceptable. . . . The ambiguity of the teaching
appears when we ask ourselves, What is good?
                        —Umberto Eco, "The Myth of Superman" (1972)

Alongside Batman, who we will consider next, Superman has been the most
enduring and impactful superhero since his origin in *Action Comics* no. 1
published in April 1938. While he was technically not the first superhero,
being predated by the likes of Mandrake (1934) and the Phantom (1936),
he was certainly the first to enter the national and even global consciousness on such a scale, and his presence looms large over the genre even
today more than eighty years later. Jerry Siegel, the cocreator of Superman,
envisioned his most famous character very much in mythological terms
as a modern day demigod, stating, "I conceived a character like Samson,
Hercules, and all the strong men I have ever heard of rolled into one," but
he could not have anticipated how much a part of contemporary American
mythology and culture the Man of Steel would become. Chris Rojek suggests that Superman has come to "represent idealized representations of
American heroism and the defence of justice."[16] Rojek's idea, concurred
with by many others, is that despite being an extraterrestrial, Superman
is an embodiment of the quintessential values that are at the center of
American national identity.
    Superman appeared in film as early as 1948, in a fifteen-part black-and-
white Columbia film serial, and then in a fifty-eight-minute long B-movie,
Superman and the Mole Men (1951), before the hugely successful, initially
at least, Christopher Reeve incarnation in *Superman* (1978), *Superman II*
(1980), *Superman III* (1983), and *Superman IV: The Quest for Peace* (1987).
Superman's opening is set in a nostalgic, vaguely 1950s setting that was
frequently evoked throughout the 1970s (see *American Graffiti* [1973] and
Grease [1978], the latter of which was the biggest box office success the
year *Superman* was released). Even the film's "present" 1970s scenes seem

far removed from the turbulent political climate of real-world America that it was produced in, and many have seen Donner's first film in the series as having resonated with audiences precisely because of this.[17] However, by the time of *Superman III* the franchise had veered so far away from the title character that it is almost as much a Richard Pryor film as it is a Superman film, and it self-destructed in *Superman IV: The Quest for Peace*, a film in which Superman is defeated more by a low budget and a terrible script than by his diegetic nemesis, Nuclear Man. The film ends with Superman returning Lex Luthor to prison and remarking, "See you in twenty," and it was just about twenty years later that he returned to the screen in *Superman Returns* (2006). While Bryan Singer's film was critically and commercially successful, earning $391 million worldwide, it did not have the impact that was expected given Superman's elevated stature in the cultural imaginary. One might have thought that this unquestionably patriotic figure would have been the perfect hero to galvanize American unity in the post-9/11 years, just as he had embodied the American spirit of resistance during the Second World War. However, Singer's old-fashioned and deeply nostalgic interpretation of the character proved an uneasy fit for a country and a globe divided by its reaction to the abuses in Abu Ghraib, the intrusions of the USA PATRIOT Act, and the ongoing wars in Iraq and Afghanistan. Soon after the genre would come to be populated with and almost exclusively defined by characters that Francis Pheasant-Kelly described as the

Fig. 2.3 The ostentatious displays of American patriotism which are a central part of *Superman II* (1980).

Fig. 2.4 The modern Superman is no longer just American, but now positioned as a global citizen in *Man of Steel* (2013).

"wounded hero," in a culture seemingly unable to accept superheroes so altruistic and flawless as Superman had been for so many years.[18]

Just seven years later those charged with bringing him back to the screen seemed aware of this, and in the three films orchestrated by Zack Snyder, *Man of Steel* (2013), *Batman v Superman: Dawn of Justice* (2016), and *Justice League* (2017), Superman is more conflicted than he had ever been, offering challenges to some of the essential tenets that have defined cinematic incarnations of the character by having him kill (albeit reluctantly) and by having his father argue that keeping his identity secret might be more important than saving innocent lives. More than this it was a lack of a coherent vision in these three films which resulted in the biggest problems. *Batman v Superman* veers between operatic portentousness, gratuitous world building (introducing Flash and Aquaman in an e-mail attachment!), ill-advised characterizations, and ethically dubious evocations of real-life culturally traumatic events. But none of this could have prepared audiences for the debacle that was *Justice League*, which for many years had been a project eagerly dreamt of by comic book fans. The final film suffers from tonal inconsistencies and numerous technical and narrative problems clearly the result of the studio losing faith in Snyder's vision after the backlash directed towards *Batman v Superman* and Joss Whedon's hastily written and unsatisfying reshoots. If someone ten years before had suggested that *Justice League*, a film that unites Superman, Batman, Wonder Woman, and Flash onscreen for the first time, might earn less at the domestic box office than *Doctor Strange* the year before and *Guardians of the Galaxy Vol. 2* the year after, it would have been unthinkable, but this is exactly what happened. The Superman films made in the first two decades of the new millennium failed to reconcile the paradoxical demands for a character updated for the modern era, while at the same time the desire for Superman to remain in essence who he always has been. Whether this can be solved in future iterations of the character or whether Superman will feature in another film worthy of his iconic legacy remains to be seen.

Case Study: Batman

> If you make yourself more than just a man, if you devote yourself to an ideal, and if they can't stop you, then you become something else entirely . . . legend, Mr. Wayne.
>
> —Henri Ducard in *Batman Begins*

> His [Batman's] appeal lies primarily in the fact that he's a human being. He's trained to the point of mental and physical perfection, but his powers are all based in human ingenuity and determination. Any reader could become Batman. Sure, you'd have to suffer a childhood trauma, inherit a fortune, hone your body, study forensics, and craft your own gadgets, but if you really put your mind to it, you could become Batman—or that's what generations of fans have told themselves.
>
> —Will Brooker, "We Could be Heroes" (2013)

With just as long and important a history as Superman, Batman has played a similarly substantial role in defining public perceptions of what a superhero is since his first appearance in *Detective Comics* no. 27 in 1939. The devotion and following he has inspired in fans, admirers, and writers has resulted in an almost uncountable number of books and articles about different facets of his character, exploring his psychology, his fluidity and potency as an evolving cultural icon, his mythic properties, his status as a

neoliberal icon, his fans, and even his sexual proclivities.[19] On the character's ability to transcend the fictional realm in a way only a few ever have,
Denis O'Neill remarks, "Although he is not real, he does have a reality,
a kind of reality he shares with mythology, folklore, legends, imaginary
friends, and (Let us lower our voices) maybe even a deity or two."[20]

Batman appeared on the cinema screen as early as 1943 in a black-
and-white fifteen-chapter serial called *The Batman* before becoming
a pop culture phenomenon as a result of the fondly remembered, pop-
art-influenced kitsch of *Batman* (ABC, 1966–1968), enjoyed as much by
adults as the children it was initially targeted at. However, it was not until
Tim Burton's darkly operatic *Batman* (1989) and *Batman Returns* (1992)
that he truly became a global cinematic icon. These were followed by two
Joel Schumacher films, the cartoonish *Batman Forever* (1995) and the
disastrous *Batman & Robin* (1997). Seven years later, Christopher Nolan
embarked upon a trilogy of Batman films, *Batman Begins* (2005), *The
Dark Knight* (2008), and *The Dark Knight Rises* (2012), widely regarded as
a benchmark for the genre and for some the defining superhero films of
the last two decades. Yet even the financial success and cultural impact
of the Nolan trilogy did not dampen the desire to bring the character to
the screen, and he was rebooted just four years later for appearances in
Batman v Superman: Dawn of Justice (2016), *Suicide Squad* (2016), and
Justice League (2017). Each of these iterations shares the essential tenets
of the character: Batman is the alter ego of the billionaire industrialist
Bruce Wayne who, as a result of his childhood trauma, prowls Gotham
City by night on a vigilante crusade, yet they each differ in various ways by
being a product of the times in which they are made either thematically,
technologically or as a result of being the artistic vision of their respective
director. As Alex M. Wainer stated in *Soul of the Dark Knight: Batman as
Mythic Figure in Comics and Film* (2014), "Throughout their handling of
the Batman feature film franchise, Warner Bros. executives have sought
directors who could contribute, not just their film-making competence but
their particular stylistic touch,"[21] whether that might be Burton's gothic
aesthetic, Nolan's War on Terror–inspired motifs, or Snyder's bombastic
cod-Nietzchean philosophizing.

Burton's tenure as director of the character results in a grandly melodramatic vision that remains striking even today, made on the cusp of the
CGI era, when actors still performed on large-scale physical sets rather

than against green screens. Burton makes no concessions at all to realism, embracing the absurdity of the character in ways antithetical to the modern superhero film, even though at the time Ron Pennington at the *Hollywood Reporter* praised *Batman* for being both "believable" and in possession of "human drama."[22] Both *Batman* and *Batman Returns* are fueled by charismatic performances by Jack Nicholson, Danny DeVito, and Michelle Pfeiffer, often leaving Batman (Michael Keaton) himself almost a secondary figure in films which bear his own name. This process continues in the Joel Schumacher years with Jim Carrey as the Riddler ("Was that over the top? I can never tell"), Tommy Lee Jones as Two-Face ("Let's start this party with a bang!"), and Arnold Schwarzenegger as Mr. Freeze ("Let's kick some ice!"). Burton quickly grew disaffected by the process, commenting of the first film, "I liked parts of it but the whole movie is mainly boring. It's OK, but it was more of a cultural phenomenon."[23] His remarks are a thinly veiled jab at the commercialization of the character and the idea that the films might be a prolonged advertisement for the accompanying retail brands, an ethos that Schumacher's tenure wholeheartedly embraced. In *Batman Forever* and *Batman & Robin* everything is exaggerated, and the screen explodes with garish colors and over-the-top performances.

Fig. 2.5 The heavily stylised characters, narrative and aesthetic of Tim Burton's *Batman* (1989).

Fig. 2.6 A Batman torn from the headlines and at war with himself as much as his enemies in *The Dark Knight*.

The Burton and Snyder films do feature the trauma that created Batman, but it is not placed in the foreground of the narrative in the ways it emphatically became in the films that followed a decade later. One of Nolan's numerous achievements is to put Batman/Bruce Wayne at the center and offer him a complete character arc—something rare in the genre. Several scholars have convincingly argued that Nolan's trilogy is immersed in and provides a compelling allegorical commentary on the War on Terror.[24] Much of the resonance of Nolan's depiction of Batman emerges from its quasi-realistic setting and context. His Gotham City is far removed from the excesses of Burton's or Schumacher's; rather, it is a grim and decidedly contemporary world with its own iconic landmark in the imposing Wayne Tower which, like the Twin Towers, comes under attack by an enigmatic terrorist, Ra's al Ghul, who is deliberately framed as a Osama bin Laden figure on a quasi-jihad-style mission to destroy Gotham City. The writer David S. Goyer made this comparison explicit when he stated, "We modelled him after Osama bin Laden. He's not crazy in the way that all the other Batman villains are. He's not bent on revenge; he's actually trying to heal the world. He's just doing it by very draconian means."[25] When Ra's al Ghul says to Batman, "You are just an ordinary man in a cape!" what is intended to be an insult in the diegetic world of the film highlights Nolan's desire to accentuate the man behind the cowl and create a believable psychological portrait of Bruce Wayne for the first time in his screen history.

Nolan's trilogy certainly allegorizes some of the defining fears and anxieties of the decade. Andrew O'Hehir wrote that Gotham is located in an America not too removed from the real one "permanently scarred in a way Osama bin Laden could only dream about."[26] While the series ultimately endorses Batman's transgressions of the law, it does offer some partial challenges, especially in *The Dark Knight*, where his need to embrace the dark side was compared by some to how Dick Cheney asserted in 2001 that many longstanding legal precedents prevented America from fighting an effective War on Terror. Cheney stated, "We also have to work, though, sort of the dark side, if you will. . . . That's the world these folks operate in, and so it's going to be vital for us to use any means at our disposal, basically, to achieve our objective."[27] Superman has historically been considered the preeminent personification of American ethics and values, but it might be more accurate to suggest that it is Batman, especially in his new millennial incarnation, who more readily encompasses the complicated and polarized post-9/11 American psyche, and this may be one of the reasons for the phenomenal success of Christopher Nolan's interpretation of the character in the decade after the attacks of September 11, 2001. While America might wish to see itself as the principled and noble Superman, in reality it resembles more closely the conflicted and much more morally ambiguous Batman. As Michael Caine, who starred as Alfred in Nolan's Batman trilogy, was said to have suggested, "Superman is the way America sees itself, but Batman is the way the world sees America."[28]

The Snyder Batman films, *Batman v Superman* and *Justice League*, as with their portrayal of Superman, present no coherent vision of Batman either. In *Batman v Superman* the film's central narrative gambit is Batman's hatred of Superman, something that is far from earned or believably portrayed onscreen; neither is the abrupt switch to understanding then admiration, motivated by the much maligned and justifiably lambasted "Martha" episode. More interesting than the film itself was how critics sought to connect it to current events, with reviews calling it "a blockbuster for the Trump era" in the run-up to the 2016 American presidential election—comments not meant to be complimentary to either party.[29] On the campaign trail Donald Trump had suggested he should be viewed as a superhero on a number of occasions: referring to himself as Batman, and in March 2016 when asked how he would be able to keep his election promises and told by one journalist, "We don't have Superman presidents," he replied "No . . . but we will if you have Trump."[30]

As Will Brooker argues in the epigraph to this case study, Batman is a wish-fulfillment figure, one grounded in the possibility that were we afforded the time, money, and circumstances, we too could *perhaps* become Batman, unlike Superman and Wonder Woman, who are far removed from human experience. It is hard to imagine what it feels like to be Superman, but can we imagine what it feels like to be Bruce Wayne? This is one of the reasons the character will probably always return to the screen in some form or another and in all likelihood will have featured in another version, if not more, by the time you have read this page.

3 GENDER AND SEXUALITY IN THE CONTEMPORARY SUPERHERO FILM

I have nothing to prove to you . . .
—Carol Danvers/Captain Marvel in *Captain Marvel*

They [superhero films] can perpetuate "traditional" ideas about gender and sexuality about race and disability by portraying stereotypes, such as, women are always weaker than men, or heterosexuality is the only acceptable form of a loving relationship, or people of color are never as capable as white people, or people with disabilities are bitter and dependent. They can also subvert those stereotypes in ways that empower those who have been marginalized because of them.
—Carolyn Cocca, *Superwomen: Gender, Power and Representation* (2016)

In perhaps the most spirited moment of many in *Captain Marvel*, the twenty-first film in the MCU and the first to have a female protagonist with her name in the title, the eponymous superhero stands face to face with the man she had thought was her friend and mentor but who has been revealed to be her nemesis, Yon-Rogg (Jude Law). He knows that she is more powerful than he is and so tries to goad her into hand-to-hand combat where at least he might have a chance . . . but she abruptly blasts him with the extraordinary energy beams she can command at will, sending him hurtling through the air landing in an ignominious heap, only pausing to add "*I have nothing to prove to you* . . . " However, as the first female-centered film in the MCU and a rare female lead in the genre, the film *did* have something to prove, which it was able to do by earning more than $1.2 billion at the global box office.

One of the primary criticisms of the superhero film has been its severely limited representation of gender and sexuality. If it is true, as this book has asserted, that the genre has both defined and shaped the contours of the contemporary Hollywood blockbuster, it also is representative of how mainstream cinema has continued to provide problematic portrayals of women and sexualities outside of those that are considered "the norm" in an era where the general consensus appears to be that there is more equality between the sexes and that media representations of gender and sexuality are more diverse than ever before. This assertion, as is the one by Cocca which provides an epigraph to this chapter, is not anecdotal, but rather supported by a range of empirical studies. What should we make of the fact that in the two decades before the release of *Captain Marvel* and *Wonder Woman* (2017), very much the period we are calling the renaissance of the genre, there had only been three other female-led superhero films: *Catwoman* (2004), *Elektra* (2005), and *My Super Ex-Girlfriend* (2006)? Or that neither Marvel, DC, nor any other company producing mainstream superhero films had provided a single non-heterosexual main or supporting character? Yet to even comment on this disparity often leads to accusations of being a "social justice warrior" or obsessed with what is pejoratively referred to as "identity politics."

The critical and commercial failures of the three female-centered films mentioned above played a considerable role in perpetuating the idea that superhero films with female leads did not and indeed could not resonate with audiences, and therefore were not wanted by general film-goers.[1] *Catwoman*, released the year before Nolan's *Batman Begins*, is one of the most high-profile commercial and critical failures in the history of the genre. Based on a character which had appeared onscreen multiple times before and even in *Batman* no. 1 (June 1940), the film "won" several Golden Raspberry awards, including Worst Picture, Worst Actress, Worst Director, and Worst Screenplay, for which its star, Halle Berry, who had received an Academy Award just a few years before for *Monster's Ball* (2001), demonstrated an admirable humility and sense of humor by attending the ceremony and accepting her award in person, adding, "I want to thank Warner Bros. Thank you for putting me in a piece of shit, god-awful movie." In the following year Jennifer Garner starred as assassin Elektra Natchios in *Elektra*, a spin-off from the underwhelming Ben Affleck vehicle *Daredevil* (2003), which struggled to fifth place at the box office even in its opening weekend. However, it is the largely forgotten 2006 movie *My Super Ex-Girlfriend*, directed by Ivan Reitman, that might be considered best representative of how the genre has historically portrayed women. The film's title reveals that even though it features a powerful female superhero, G-Girl (and her alter ego, Jenny Johnson), played by a big star (Uma Thurman, who had played Poison Ivy in *Batman & Robin* ten years before), it is not actually her story at the center of the narrative; rather, it is that of her partner, Matthew (Luke Wilson). G-Girl is intelligent and strong and has powers similar to Superman's but is dubiously portrayed with mental health issues connected to her gender and is described by other characters as a "nutcase," "neurotic," and a "complete emotional basket case" in ways that one hopes would be regarded as problematic by contemporary audiences. Matthew's masculinity is challenged by having a partner with such prodigious abilities, remarking "I'm feeling just a little bit *emasculated* . . . " even as the camera continues to linger over G-Girl's form-fitting costume in scene after scene. Matthew certainly can be regarded as a substitute for studio executives of the era, concerned whether cinemagoers would be inclined to pay money to see a superhero film with a female lead. In the film's climax Matthew's new partner, Hannah (Ana Faris), is also given superpowers solely so that the film's men, and presumably those in the audience, can see her and G-Girl fight. If *My Super Ex-Girlfriend* had been one of many superhero films to feature women made in the period, it would hardly be worth discussing, but as one of only three released throughout the whole of the decade its significance is magnified, as is the pattern it embodies of relegating the stories of women to the margins of the frame. In similar ways to this, but in much better films: *Guardians of the Galaxy* is Peter Quill's story not Gamora's; *Hancock* is Hancock's story not Mary Embrey's; and *The Avengers* and its sequels are a story about Captain America, Iron Man, and Thor much more than they are ever about Black Widow.

There are interesting female characters in these years: Black Widow, Scarlet Witch, Hit Girl, Teenage Negasonic Warhead, Liz Sherman, Gamora,

Domino, and Storm, but none of them is at the center of the films they feature in, and they have tended to be secondary characters by quite some margin, frequently defined by their vulnerability, whether that is physical, psychological or emotional, in ways that male superheroes rarely are. So, for example, in the original X-Men trilogy, comprised of *X-Men* (2002), *X-Men 2* (2003), and *X-Men: The Last Stand* (2006), there are plenty of female characters—the aforementioned Storm, Mystique, Jean Grey, Rogue—but none is ever the driving force of the narrative, which is emphatically about the experiences of three men: Wolverine (Hugh Jackman), Professor X (Patrick Stewart), and Magneto (Ian McKellen). In the second iteration of the franchise, the prequels *X-Men: First Class* (2011), *X-Men: Days of Future Past* (2014), *X-Men: Apocalypse* (2016), and *Dark Phoenix* (2019), this focus changed somewhat, with Jennifer Lawrence's Mystique being almost as important to the narrative as the new versions of Professor X and Magneto, now played by James McAvoy and Michael Fassbender, respectively, yet the newer films still feature numerous female characters, like Storm, Emma Frost, Angel Salvadore, and Blink, whose primary function seems to be to look attractive and whose powers are often connected to their appearance, femininity, and sexuality. In the closing film of the prequel series, *Dark Phoenix*, Jean Grey (Sophie Turner) is the eponymous main character, but again the film is less about her than about how the men around her react to her newly acquired otherworldly powers. Unpersuasive attempts to connect the film to contemporary dimensions of gender discourse result in awkward moments, such as when Mystique confronts Professor X with the line, "By the way, the women are always saving the men around here; you might want to think about changing the name to X-Women!"

Outside of those with superpowers, women in the genre like Lois Lane ("You smell good"), Rachel Dawes ("I don't understand any of this"), Jane Foster ("I like how you explain things"), Betty Ross ("Bruce, I don't understand why we can't just walk in and talk to my father"), and Pepper Potts ("Who's the hot mess now?") are given important professions (Pulitzer Prize–winning journalist, lawyer, astrophysicist, cellular biologist, and CEO, respectively), but they still tend to function, as in the majority of mainstream blockbusters, as either victims to be saved, or rewards for the heroism of their superhero male partners, who in every single example listed above also give the films their names. In this way we can observe that the contemporary superhero film promotes a shallow level of female empowerment, at the same time as continuing to participate in their marginalization and objectification. This results in films which consistently fail to pass what is referred to as the Bechdel test, named after the cartoonist Alison Bechdel, which, simply put, requires that a film must contain two named female characters who talk about something other than a male character. As unscientific a barometer as the Bechdel test is, it provides a testimony to the fact female characters rarely occupy the privileged and dynamic spaces of the genre and tend to be marginalized at best or objectified, sexualized, and infantilized at worst.

These observations are supported by a range of empirical studies conducted by a diverse range of institutions and individuals who have conducted research in this area, the most prominent of which are those undertaken by the Media, Diversity, and Social Change Initiative at USC Annenberg's School for Communication and Journalism, the Geena Davis Institute on Gender in Media, and the Center for the Study of Women in Television and Film, who each come to the same conclusions and provide statistical evidence in support. Their research indicates that on average, taking into account the one hundred top-grossing films of the year, women occupy only 28–33 percent of speaking roles. In the action and adventure genres (which include the superhero film) this decreases to closer to 20 percent. Women are considerably more likely than men to be shown in sexy attire (27.9 vs. 8 percent), featured nude (26.4 vs. 9.1 percent), or referred to as physically attractive (12.6 vs. 3.1 percent).[2] Additionally, the 2017 USC Annenberg study "Inclusion in the Director's Chair? Gender, Race, and Age of Film Directors Across 1,000 Films from 2007–2016" revealed that there are almost twenty-four male directors for every one female director in Hollywood, that female directors' careers are not as long as those of men, and that they are overwhelmingly offered dramas rather than other genres.[3] Considering one particular year in detail, 2017, a year in which five superhero films occupied the top ten domestic box office—*Wonder Woman, Guardians of the Galaxy Vol.2, Spider-Man: Homecoming, Thor: Ragnarok*, and *Justice League*—women constituted 24 percent of protagonists in the 100 top domestic grossing films and 34 percent of all speaking characters. Just 32 percent of films featured ten or more female characters in speaking roles; in sharp contrast to this, 79 percent had ten or more male characters with speaking roles. Female characters remained younger than the men, as they always have, with the majority of female characters in their twenties (32 percent) or thirties (25 percent) but the majority of men in their thirties (31 percent) or forties (27 percent).[4]

Thus examples like *Wonder Woman* in 2017 and *Captain Marvel* in 2019 are understandably held up as significant examples of diversity and progress, which they are, but they are rare exceptions rather than developing trends. *Captain Marvel*, the twenty-first film in the MCU, but the first with a female superhero named in the title and the first with a female director, in this case codirector Anna Boden, is an interesting film and indeed a powerful one, but the burden of being Marvel's first female-centered cinematic outing and self-consciously constructed as a "feminist text" is a heavy one on its narrative. Furthermore, its feminism is shrewdly calculated, designed first and foremost to sell tickets and participate in a social movement that neither Marvel nor Disney had shown any interest in until it became financially profitable to do so. This is not to say that Carol Danvers's story does not entertain or inspire: her journey toward becoming her true self features intergalactic combat between rival alien species, but her plight is a very human one that resonates with women, young or old, who have been told they are *too emotional* by men seeking to define who they are and what they can do. This is something Carol is told many times throughout the film: "There's nothing more dangerous for a warrior than emotions"; "You struggle with your emotions"; and "Do not let your emotions override your judgment." Yet in having to be representative of so much the filmmakers choose heavy-handedness over subtlety almost every time, including simplistic musical choices like the primarily female 1990s music on the soundtrack, especially the egregious use of No Doubt's "Just a Girl" (1995) at its climax. When its star Brie Larson spoke out fairly innocuously about the lack of diversity in front of and behind the camera during the publicity tour for the film, her comments became the target of outraged internet campaigners, who posted negative reviews for *Captain Marvel* even before its release in an attempt to affect its box office success; these protesters justified their actions with statements like "Tired of all this SJW nonsense." The film was described by online fringe groups as "feminist propaganda" or as possessing a "hard pro-leftist agenda."[5] This is just one more example that films are only regarded as "political," using the term as a pejorative, when they do not adhere to one's own

Fig. 3.1 The protagonist of *Captain Marvel* (2019) might have declared, "I have nothing to prove to you," but the film demonstrated that audiences would turn out in record numbers to see female protagonists in a genre that has been historically defined by male superheroes.

political views. For some, as incredible as it might seem, it is *not political* that twenty-two of the films in the first three phases of the MCU feature men in the title and leading roles, nor is it political that women are pushed to the margins of the screen and are rarely afforded the narrative centrality of their male counterparts in the superhero genre.

Alongside these very valid criticisms of the genre, others have targeted the lack of diversity in the sexualities of the protagonists and supporting characters in superhero films. As with representations of gender, we live in an era which is widely considered to be defined as more open than ever concerning matters of sexual identity, but there is very little evidence of this in the film industry and in particular in the superhero film. The super-hero genre, both historically and currently, is *exclusively* heteronormative; in the first twenty-one MCU films there was not a single example of a non-heterosexual character. In the industry as a whole, empirical studies conducted by GLAAD reported that only 12.8 percent of the 109 movies released from major studios in 2017 included a LGBTQ character, and there were no transgender characters in any major studio release. The follow-ing year in GLAAD's annual "Studio Responsibility Index," which assigns a grade for issues of representation to the seven major studios concern-ing, all received "poor" or "failing" except 20th Century Fox and Universal, who were deemed "insufficient." On the superhero genre specifically the report lamented,

> There are so many LGBTQ heroes in comics—enough for GLAAD to up its Outstanding Comic Book award category from five to ten nominees to reflect the quality and quantity of what we are seeing— that it is becoming increasingly more difficult to ignore that LGBTQ people remain almost completely shut out of Hollywood's big budget comic films. There have been several films in recent years that have erased a character's queer identity as they moved from page to screen. In 2017, Marvel's *Thor: Ragnarok* [Valkyrie and Korg] and DC's *Wonder Woman* both included characters who are queer in the source material, but did not include any on screen confirmation of their identities. This must change going forward.[6]

When asked about this, James Gunn, writer/director of *Guardians of the Galaxy* and *Guardians of the Galaxy Vol. 2*, offered an answer with a rather tortuous relationship to logic: "There's a lot of characters in the MCU and very few of them have we delved into what their sexuality is [*sic*], whether it's gay or straight or bisexual, we don't really know. So, I imagine that there are probably, you know, gay characters in the Marvel Universe we just don't know who they are yet."[7] The "very few" that Gunn is talking about cannot include the likes of Tony Stark (Iron Man), Bruce Banner (Hulk), Thor, Steve Rogers (Captain America), Natasha Romanov (Black Widow), Clint Barton (Hawkeye), Scott Lang (Ant-Man), Peter Quill, Gamora, Drax, or Yondu Udonta (Guardians of the Galaxy), all of whom are shown to be clearly heterosexual—as is *every single character* that is seen in a romantic relationship onscreen, not just on Earth but *all over the galaxy* in the MCU that Gunn initially contributed to, and also in the DCEU, where Gunn later moved to write and direct *The Suicide Squad* (2021).

Just as the Bechdel test provides audiences with an informal and imperfect but always interesting way of seeing how any given film portrays women, many have now begun to turn to the "Vito Russo test," which takes its name from the celebrated film historian and GLAAD cofounder Vito Russo, whose book *The Celluloid Closet* (1981) remains as essential today as it was when first published more than thirty years ago. To pass the Vito Russo test a film must contain at least one character that is identifiably lesbian, gay, bisexual, or transgender, and that character cannot be exclusively defined by their sexual orientation or gender identity: they must exist as central to the plot in some fashion. Yet even with these fairly loose criteria not a single film in the MCU or the DCEU passes, and, debatably, only *Deadpool 2* in the whole mainstream genre. Technically, *Avengers: Endgame* featured the first gay character in the MCU when another Russo, Joe Russo, the movie's codirector, appeared in a minor role credited only as "grieving man." He described it as "important to us as we did four of these films, we wanted a gay character somewhere in them. We felt it was important that one of us play him, to ensure the integrity and show it is so important to the filmmakers that one of us is representing that. It is a perfect time, because one of the things that is compelling about the Marvel Universe moving forward is its focus on diversity." Others less charitably and more accurately called it "a half-baked attempt at diversity."[8]

Those wanting more than heteronormativity from the genre have had to look for it in subtext or allegory or even create it on their own. For example, many writers have convincingly argued that the struggle for mutant identity

Fig. 3.2 Negasonic Teenage Warhead and Yukio in *Deadpool 2* (2018), the first gay superheroes shown in a relationship in the history of genre in a mainstream superhero film.

in the X-Men film franchise can be interpreted as a plea for tolerance for different sexualities and that many of its creators intended for it to be read this way. Lisa Purse writes, "Like homosexuals the mutants are forced to establish safe spaces like Xavier's school where they can be themselves and express their tendencies without censure."[9] Indeed, there are many moments that leap from the screen and demand to be read in such a way, in particular, the scene in *X-Men* when Iceman/Bobby Drake (Shawn Ashmore) reveals to his parents that he is a mutant in dialogue positively laden with subtext, as in when his mother asks him "Have you tried . . . not being a mutant?" Though this allegorical reading of the series is powerful, it cannot take the place of *real representation*, and at the time of writing, after more than ten X-Men films there has not been a single explicitly gay character.

Adding to this, even characters who are gay in the comic book source material are often rewritten to be heterosexual in the film adaptations: like Valkyrie (Tessa Thompson) and Korg (Taika Waititi) in *Thor: Ragnarok*, Ayo (Florence Kasumba) in *Black Panther*, and Psylocke (Olivia Munn) in *X-Men: Apocalypse*. Some of these actors imply or outright announce to fans that their characters are not heterosexual, but ultimately the final films released at multiplexes all around the globe feature none of this onscreen. While Deadpool is widely referred to as "pansexual" with the character's cocreator Fabian Nicieza stating, "Deadpool is whatever sexual inclination his brain tells him he is in THAT moment. And then the moment passes,"[10] the cinematic incarnation offers no such fluidity: he is provided with a girlfriend, Vanessa (Morena Baccarin), to love, rescue on multiple occasions, and mourn when she dies in *Deadpool 2* in a fairly explicit example of "fridging," a term coined by the writer Gail Simone to describe a habitual process in the genre whereby female characters are raped, killed, or depowered as little more than a plot device to propel the action forward and center the narrative around the hero. As of 2018 the only notable gay character in the superhero genre was Negasonic Teenage Warhead (Brianna Hildebrand), who is shown with her partner, Yukio (Shiori Kutsuna), in *Deadpool 2*, although they are hardly central to the plot and Deadpool's only real reference to them is calling them "a super cute couple." In this climate fans often create their own narratives about non-heterosexual characters and relationships. So while fan fiction often details, as Francesca Coppa writes, who "would win in a fight, Captain America or Superman, and they don't care that one of these characters comes from Marvel and one from DC," it also frequently explores possible romantic bonds between characters like Steve Rogers and Bucky Barnes, Bruce Wayne and Clark Kent, or Black Widow and Gamora.[11]

In 2015 Kevin Feige suggested that "there's no reason" the MCU could not include an LGBTQ character "in the next decade or sooner." [12] And in July 2019 at Comic-Con he announced that *Thor: Love and Thunder* would feature the franchise's first openly gay main character, Tessa Thompson's Valkyrie, and that the film would also see the return of Natalie Portman playing not only Jane Foster but also a female Thor as the character has been portrayed in recent versions of the comics. For many in the audience and those around the world, it was about time.

Case Study: Wonder Woman

I am the man who can . . .
—Wonder Woman in *Wonder Woman* (2017)

Diana is an inherently political character—she's about feminist politics, humanist politics, sex politics, the politics of war etc.—and that fact is probably her downfall. What makes her fascinating and endearing to me is also what makes her controversial and unlikeable to some; it's also one of the things that make her such a difficult property commercially.
—Marc DiPaolo, *War, Politics, and Superheroes: Ethics and propaganda in Comics and Film* (2011)

The very fact that Wonder Woman, one of the quintessential figures in the superhero pantheon, a character who has been in publication continuously since her debut in *All Star Comics* no. 8 (October 1941) and was the star of a fondly remembered television series (ABC/CBS, 1975–79), took seventy-six years to make it to the screen should be regarded as evidence to support many of the assertions contained previously in this chapter concerning the reluctance of the industry to make superhero films featuring female protagonists. We might ask why *Blankman* (1994), *The Phantom* (1996), *Steel* (1997), *Ghost Rider* (2007), or even *Ant-Man* (2015) and *Doctor Strange* (2016), before a film featuring the iconic figure of Wonder Woman?

Finally released in 2017, *Wonder Woman*—directed by Patty Jenkins, the first high profile female director of a film from the genre—became a cultural phenomenon not just in terms of its financial success, which was indeed considerable, but how it was received by audiences all around the globe as a lightning rod for debates concerning the way women are portrayed in the genre, but also beyond the frames of the screen in discourse which prefigured the #MeToo and Time's Up movements. This reception of the film could be observed in the multitude of contemporaneous editorials and opinion pieces which appeared with titles like "Why *Wonder Woman* Is a Masterpiece of Subversive Feminism," "Why Wonder Woman Is the Perfect Hero for the Trump era," and "Wonder Woman in the Age of Trump."[13] The character's appropriation and use in feminist discourse is ironic given that she has featured was created in 1941 by William Moulton Marston (under the pen name of Charles Mouton) as an explicit if problematic symbol of feminine power and featured in debates concerning these matters since her creation. About her comic book incarnation, Fredric Wertham wrote in his *Seduction of the Innocent* that she "is physically very powerful, tortures men, has her own female following, is the cruel 'phallic' woman. While she is a frightening figure for boys, she is an undesirable figure for girls, being the exact opposite of what girls are supposed to be." However writers like Ruth McClelland-Nugent praise her for many of the same reasons, regarding her as "powerful and self-reliant, hailing from a peaceful, female-centred society, she represented many values that deeply resonated with Second Wave Feminism." And no less a cultural arbiter than Gloria Steinem writes, "If we had all read more about Wonder Woman and less about Dick and Jane . . . the new wave of the feminist revolution might have happened less painfully and sooner."[14] This is a substantial amount of baggage for what many might regard as *just a superhero movie*. The resulting film is a problematic one, certainly a rip-roaring and emotionally engaging addition to the genre, but as DiPaolo asserts in the epigraph to this case study, Wonder Woman's inherently political nature becomes diluted in a variety of ways to mediate the fact that she might be "a difficult property commercially" were she to remain the character as originally envisioned and explored so often throughout the course of her history in the comic books.

Thus, for the most part *Wonder Woman* in superhero blockbuster mode reverts to simplistic platitudes with its First World War period setting providing a convenient distance to contemporary debates in the same way

Fig. 3.3 Despite being in print continuously since her comic book debut in 1941, Wonder Woman did not appear in a feature film until Gal Gadot portrayed her.

Captain America: The First Avenger was able to mediate some of the jingo-ism of its title character. Like the Second World War setting of *The First Avenger*, the war to end all wars in *Wonder Woman* is one-dimensional and mythologized, content to embrace Steve Trevor's assertion that as an American he is "one of the good guys and those [pointing at the Germans] are the bad guys." The film portrays the Germans and the Ottoman Empire as creators of a new form of deadly gas, embodying an erroneous con-tention that World War I was a noble war fought for justice and freedom, not the complicated geopolitical enterprise of rivalry for land, influence, and economic interest that it actually was. Its Germans become framed as Nazis, with even the odd reviewer forgetting and calling them just that.[15] It is critical of the war and many of those in the high command of the British Army; in one of its most powerful scenes Diana challenges those who would send hundreds of thousands to their deaths with the stroke of a pen, telling them, "You would knowingly sacrifice all their lives as if they mean less than yours!" It is also a rare superhero film that portrays civil-ian casualties in the acknowledged but offscreen deaths of the innocent Belgian civilians killed by poison gas. The genre has historically refused to allow that its heroes would permit such a thing to happen, even while destroying huge swaths of landscape and buildings at the same time.

The period setting also allows the film more freedom to explore explicitly framed gender politics as Wonder Woman chafes against the established role of women at the time ("What do these women wear into battle?"; "Where I'm from that's called slavery"), but these issues are placed safely in the distant past, allowing audiences to feel secure in the knowledge of how far we have moved on since then. Diana/Wonder Woman is provided with a love interest who has considerably more screen time and agency than the women who accompany male superheroes on their adventures. Chris Pine's Steve Trevor is a hero in his own right, goes on numerous missions, and has his own heroic moment of sacrifice, usually given only to protagonists. This is far from the treatment of characters like Lois Lane in the DCEU, Jane Foster in *Thor*, Pepper Potts in *Iron Man*, and Christine Palmer in *Doctor Strange* and not too dissimilar from any of Pine's other heroic leading-man roles such as Captain Kirk in the *Star Trek* franchise (2009–) or Jack Ryan in *Jack Ryan: Shadow Recruit* (2014), even though Wonder Woman is shown to rescue him numerous times through the film.

The film's most remarkable sequences are in its prologue, set in Themyscira, the idyllic all-female world ruled by Diana's mother Hippolyta (Connie Nielsen) and its most able warrior, her aunt Antiope (Robyn Wright), populated by multiracial women who have never even seen a man before. Yet in this society the film implies non-heterosexuality only twice: once in a humorous fashion, when Diana tells Steve, "I've read all twelve volumes of Clio's treatises on bodily pleasure," concluding that "men are essential for procreation but when it comes to pleasure, unnecessary," and once in a look exchanged between Antiope and one of her fellow soldiers. On release it was embraced by many as "a masterpiece of subversive feminism" with the new iteration of the character a "feminist role model for an age of resistance." For some though, as one might expect, its politics went too far, and Josephine Livingstone at the *New Republic* was one of many to call it "propaganda" and the bearer of "empty feminist platitudes."[16] It is too early to say whether *Wonder Woman* marked the start of a new relationship between the genre and women, but it comprehensively challenged the idea that audiences do not want female-led superhero films by making more money at the box office than both *Justice League* and *Batman v Superman*, something that would have been hard to predict just a few years before,

Fig. 3.4 Sharing screen time with her love interest in ways male superheroes are never asked to do in *Wonder Woman*.

and paved the way for an eagerly awaited sequel also directed by Patty Jenkins, *Wonder Woman 1984* (2020), as the superhero renaissance moved confidently into its third decade showing no signs of slowing down.

Case Study: The Incredibles

> Leave the saving of the world to the men? I don't think so. . . .
> —Helen Parr/Mrs. Incredible in *The Incredibles* (2004)

> On the big screen, superheroes have stood for a few different notions—the outcasts of X-Men, the exultant empowerment avatars of *Wonder Woman* and *Black Panther*, the chill workplace family of The Avengers, the persecution-complex ubermenschen of *Batman v Superman*. In *Incredibles 2*, superheroes stand for—well, all of that. . . . Bird's made the weirdest Pixar movie ever, revolutionary and retro, an anti-authoritarian ode to good parenting.
> —Darren Franich, *Entertainment Weekly* (2018)

Brad Bird's *The Incredibles* (2004) is one of the first films in what I have referred to as the renaissance period of the superhero genre and an early

Pixar release made during the time it seemed as if the company could do no wrong, part of a string of commercial and critical successes that saw it go from being purchased for $5 million by Steve Jobs in 1986 to being bought by Disney in 2006 for $7.4 billion.[17] The timing of the first film was propitious, after Sam Raimi's *Spider-Man* (2002) but before the genre's veristic turn, and it is a text that affectionately satirizes the superhero film while embracing many of its central tropes in ways that seem fresh and dynamic even now.

The Incredibles and its sequel follow a family of superheroes, the Parrs, dramatizing an element that would become key to the modern superhero film: the struggle to live their lives as ordinary people while dealing with the responsibilities that their powers bring.[18] They are a rare new addition to the pantheon of the genre given that the vast majority of the superhero films released are adapted from comic books. Yet even though they are original, their characters and the powers they possess correspond to some of the genre's enduring archetypes, evoking many of its iconic characters. Bob Parr/Mr. Incredible is on the surface one of the chisel-jawed, barrel-chested superheroes that we have come to expect from the genre, yet in a twist on the archetypal super man, his confidence and self-belief are sometimes shown to be reckless. Bob's wife, Helen Parr/Elastigirl is able to stretch her body into impossible shapes and in the first film is a stay at home mother looking after her three children: the teenage Violet, who can turn invisible and manipulate energy fields; the preteen Dash, who can move at incredible speeds; and the baby, Jack Jack, with powers that are unknown until the final moments of the first film and who in the sequel emerges as super in ways beyond what his family are able to imagine. Brad Bird asserts that their powers should be considered intimately connected to their characters in a strikingly direct manifestation of Coogan's "powers, identity, mission" template: "Men are always expected to be strong, so I had Bob have super strength. Women, mothers are always pulled in a million different directions, so I had her be elastic. Teenagers are insecure and defensive, so I had Violet have force fields and invisibility. Ten-year-olds are energy balls that can't be stopped. And babies are unknown."[19]

The Parrs exist in a vaguely 1950s setting evidenced by its period era cars and radios, very much retro-future in design which provides both a vivid backdrop and also a pervasive sense of nostalgia. Importantly, in their world the government enforces a law known as the Superhero

Relocation Act, which was supported by 85 percent of the public and makes superheroic activities illegal. The reasons for this are effectively drama-tized in the film's prologue when Bob saves someone about to commit suicide who then proceeds to sue him and the government for intervening. This is not the only time heroes have been regulated in comics or in films: in *Watchmen* (2009) a central element was the Keene Act, which made costumed vigilantism illegal; the Sokovia Accords provided the plot device in *Captain America: Civil War*; and perhaps most importantly in the X-Men franchise, where the Mutant Registration Act enforces the registration of every mutant.

While the film is about the Parr family—they are, after all, the Incredi-bles of the film's title—it is primarily Bob's story as he is undergoing the superhero version of a midlife crisis. It is him the film follows at night secretly saving people while pretending to go bowling with his old friend Frozone (Samuel L. Jackson) and Helen stays at home with the children. The film takes little interest in whether she is fulfilled by this, resulting in a narrative in which the "rebelliousness of Mr. Incredible and Dash smacks of privilege to which the other characters do not have access. Is it not equally unfair that Frozone and Elastigirl are deprived of using their powers

Fig. 3.5 They might be a family, but *The Incredibles* (2004) is really the story of Bob/Mr. Incredible more than anyone else who shares the screen with him.

for recognition and serving the public welfare?"[20] Thus *The Incredibles*, as many in the genre do, offers witty deconstructions of many aspects of the superhero film with its comments about how unsuitable capes are for superheroes and how bad guys love to monologue, but at the same time it perpetuates what Dietmar Meinel describes in his *Pixar's America: The Re-Animation of American Myths and Symbols* (2018) as "normative notions of femininity and masculinity with . . . gendered divisions of public and private spaces."[21]

It is Bob who we are sutured to, it is him who we are positioned to identify with, being frequently placed directly in his shoes as he trains and recovers his libido, we even learn about the (supposed) death of his family exactly as he does. When he becomes rejuvenated the film takes a joyous turn, and it is no surprise it is coded like an affair in a montage where he gets slimmer, fitter and stronger, with all Helen being required to do is look on. Later his excuse for not wanting Helen to go on adventures is the one used by many men in the genre "I can't lose you," repeated almost verbatim by Hank Pym (Michael Douglas) to his daughter Hope (Evangeline Lilly) in *Ant-Man*, before reluctantly allowing her to become the Wasp in *Ant-Man and the Wasp*.

In the fourteen years that passed between the first film and *Incredibles 2* there had been many changes in the superhero genre and indeed the world we have periodically seen it both reflect and engage with, even though the second film continues just moments after the first ended. The sequel's background is once again public attitudes toward superheroes: when a wealthy pro-superhero businessman, Winston Devour, wants a figurehead to enable him to sway the public's attitude against the Superhero Relocation Act he chooses Helen, to Bob's disbelief. She is reluctant ("I don't know" . . . "Not a good time to be away"), but the family is facing financial problems, another element rarely touched on in the genre, so they decide she will go to work while Bob stays at home with the children. This set-up places Helen at the film's center instead of Bob, but unlike in the first film the domestic sphere now proves of interest to Brad Bird with Bob's attempts to be a stay at home dad.

Devour chooses Helen over Bob for very modern reasons pertaining to contemporary society and to the superhero film. Helen is preferable because of the destruction Bob tends to leave in his wake, something the genre began to have a dialogue with itself about, as we have seen, in the

Fig. 3.6 Fourteen years after the first film, Mrs. Incredible takes center stage in
The Incredibles 2 (2018).

modern era. Her initial hesitancy is soon replaced by a sense of achieve-
ment and the difference she is able to make to the citizens of Metroville,
while Bob is left to fight a different type of battle on the home front, the
likes of which she had dealt with for years. As a returning Edna remarks,
"Done properly, parenting is a heroic act"—with the audience perhaps
aware of the fact that no such assertion, dialogue or scenes were used
during the first film when Helen was at home with the children.

In the first film the antagonist had been Buddy, a.k.a. Syndrome, an
entitled fan seeking revenge after being rejected by Mr. Incredible, antici-
pating a trend in pop culture that was to emerge frequently in the years
after, but the second film features Screenslaver, who incorporates contemporary criticisms of the genre into her monologue: "Superheroes are
part of your brainless desire to replace true experience with simulation. . . .
Every meaningful experience must be packaged and delivered to you to
watch at a distance so that you can remain ever sheltered, ever ravenous
consumers."

As with *Captain Marvel* and *Wonder Woman*, the film found itself
targeted by those not satisfied with the idea of putting a woman at the
center of a superhero film, as if doing so is an example of agenda-based
identity politics rather than diversity. These complaints were typified by
the likes of a Twitter user who wrote, "Tried to relive my childhood by
seeing *Incredibles 2* yesterday. The movie would have been fine if there
wasn't an agenda. Very modern feminist movie. Leave politics out of

73

cartoons and children's movies. Bad enough it's all you hear now, but kids [*sic*] movies?!? COME ON."[22] What this critic fails to recognize is that *every film is political*, not just those which challenge one's own political perspectives but also those that perpetuate them . . . even those used to sell toys, lunchboxes and Happy Meals—and perhaps *especially* when they are.

4 ETHNICITY IN THE CONTEMPORARY SUPERHERO FILM

Oh, so it's back to pretending we're human again? C'mon . . . spare
me the Uncle Tom routine, okay? You can't keep denying what you
are, man. You think the humans will ever accept a half-breed like
you? They can't. They're afraid of you. And they should be. You're
an animal!

—Deacon Frost in *Blade* (1998)

Accepting stereotypes is a fact of filmic life, the presence of a particular stereotype is not evidence of racism as such. It is the persistence and durability of stereotypes over time which will determine
to what degree there has been progress.

—Eugene Franklin Wong, *On Visual Media Racism:
Asians in the American Motion Pictures* (1978)

In Adilifu Nama's indispensable monograph *Super Black: American Pop
Culture and Black Superheroes* (2011), the author charts the history of the
representation of black superheroes, primarily in comic books, throughout the second half of the twentieth century, with notable examples like
Black Panther (first appearance in July 1966), Falcon (September 1969),
Luke Cage (June 1972), and Spawn (May 1992). Nama proposes that these
figures offered African Americans varied images of black heroes in eras that
were frequently defined by racial turbulence. Nama reserves just a single

chapter for African American cinematic superheroes, for the simple reason that they have been so infrequent and so disappointing, both before the period we have described as the renaissance and during it. In the decade before the release of *Black Panther* in February 2018 there was only a single high-profile superhero film with a black actor as the lead, *Hancock* (2008), starring Will Smith. Going back even further does little to alter this; in the ten years before *Hancock* there is only the commercial and critical disaster that was the Halle Berry vehicle *Catwoman* (2004) and Wesley Snipes as Blade in the trilogy of *Blade* (1998), *Blade II* (2002), and *Blade Trinity* (2004): twenty years of the superhero genre with few enough films with black leads to count on the fingers of one hand.[1] As problematic as this is, the situation concerning the representation of other ethnic minorities is even worse *and* written about less frequently. Pause for a moment and try to name superheroes of Asian, Hispanic, and Arab descent who have been part of the superhero cinematic renaissance. While these ethnic groups make up a significant portion of the United States, a combined 37.3 percent according to the 2017 census, and an even greater proportion of the world at large, at the time of writing not a single superhero film has featured one as a lead, co-lead, or even a major character. It was not until the announcement that phase 4 of the MCU would feature the Chinese martial artist Shang Chi in *Shang-Chi and the Legend of the Ten Rings* (2021) that the superhero film had its first Asian protagonist.

In this respect there are distinct parallels between these problems and the issues explored in the previous chapter concerning the representation of women and non-heteronormative sexualities, even though it is regarded as a truism that we live in an age of increasing diversity. One empirical study into the topic led by Dr. Stacy L. Smith at the University of Southern California as part of the Annenberg Inclusion Initiative, looked at films from a span of eleven years and found that in 2017 only 12.1 percent of speaking characters in the top one hundred films were black, the lowest figure since 2012, and that 2011 was the smallest proportion in the time studied at 9.1 percent. For women of color the statistics were even more disheartening, with forty-three of the top hundred films released in 2017 featuring no black female characters *at all*. The study concludes with a quote which the authors choose to present in bold for emphasis: "Overall, the findings reveal that no meaningful change has occurred in the percentage of Black/African American, Hispanic/Latino, Asian, or Mixed Race/Other characters during the years studied."[2] This disparity continues behind the camera; across the eleven years and 1,100 films studied, only 5.2 percent were helmed by a black/African American director. For the superhero genre, in the first eleven years of the MCU—twenty-two films—only four as were written or directed by a person of color: Taika Waititi directed *Thor: Ragnarok*; Hawk Ostby cowrote *Iron Man*; and Joe Robert Cole and Ryan Coogler cowrote *Black Panther*, with Coogler directing.

The true impact of these issues of representation is hard to quantify, although the USC Annenberg studies suggest they are considerable. Jamil Smith, writing about *Black Panther* in a *Time* article entitled "The Revolutionary Power of Black Panther," argues that it can be profound:

If you are reading this and you are white, seeing people who look like you in mass media probably isn't something you think about often. Every day, the culture reflects not only you but nearly infinite versions of you—executives, poets, garbage collectors, soldiers, nurses and so on. The world shows you that your possibilities are boundless. Now, after a brief respite, you again have a President. Those of us who are not white have considerably more trouble not only finding representation of ourselves in mass media and other arenas of public life, but also finding representation that indicates that our humanity is multifaceted. Relating to characters onscreen is necessary not merely for us to feel seen and understood, but also for others who need to see and understand us. When it doesn't happen, we are all the poorer for it.[3]

In the case of black superheroes in film there have been some, but they are almost always secondary characters like Falcon, War Machine and Frozone, best friends and sidekicks to the white superheroes whose name is the same as the title of the films they feature in, or pushed to the side of narratives, like Cyborg seemingly erased from what might have been a compelling character in *Justice League*, or Nick Fury, an imposing presence across the MCU but very rarely a character at the center of the drama. The 1990s featured five superhero films with black leads: *The Meteor Man* (1993), *Blankman* (1994), *Steel* (1997), *Spawn* (1997) and *Blade* (1998); Nama describes the first three as the "most questionable cinematic representations of black superheroes ever presented."[4] It is the latter, the

Fig. 4.1 Wesley Snipes as the eponymous lead in *Blade* (1998): a rare superhero film with a nonwhite actor as protagonist.

first of Wesley Snipes' Blade trilogy which offers the most interesting black superhero before the renaissance; indeed, *Blade* is another contender for marking the beginning of the return of the superhero film, with its grittier aesthetic showcased in its thrilling nightclub opening sequence, its rich mythology, and the fact that it takes the genre more seriously than films like *Batman & Robin* and *The Phantom* (1996), released just two years before.

As already mentioned, the situation is considerably worse for representation of other ethnic groups, such as Asians, Hispanics, and Arabs, both in the superhero genre and in American film as a whole. Only 6.3 percent of characters in the top one hundred films of 2017 were Asian. Thirty-seven of these films had no Asian characters at all; twenty had no black characters; and forty-three had no Hispanics. The figures for women from racial minorities are even more depressing: forty-three had no black women; sixty-four had no Hispanic women; and sixty-five no Asian women. Furthermore, when Asian, Hispanic, or Arab characters do feature they tend to be marginalized or heavily stereotyped. Just as many comic book superheroes are black, many others are Asian like, including Amadeus Cho, Jubilee, Cassandra Cain (Batgirl), Silk, Kamala Khan (Ms. Marvel), and Xombi, but few of these will be familiar to general audiences as they have not been featured in films and there was not an Asian lead in a superhero film in the first two decades of the new millennium. The closest we get are supporting characters: Wong in *Doctor Strange*, Hogun in *Thor*, Jim Morita in *Captain America: The First Avenger*, Helen Cho in *Avengers: Age of Ultron*, Ned in *Spider-Man Homecoming*, or Mantis in *Guardians of the Galaxy*. This is evidence of Hollywood's "rocky history when it comes to its portrayals of Asian Americans, from the early yellow-face roles to the still-present examples of whitewashing," which went largely uncommented on the mainstream media for decades but now at least is being discussed more frequently.[5] When Asian cultures are featured in the genre, in films like *Doctor Strange* (2016) or television shows like *Iron Fist* (Netflix, 2017–18), they are seen exclusively through the eyes of a privileged Western male, who without exception prove themselves physically, intellectually, and morally superior to their Asian counterparts. The same issues affect the representations of Hispanic characters. Many exist in print, including Ghost Rider, White Tiger, Firebird, Miss America, and Blue Beetle, but very few of these find their way to the screens and if they do they are almost

Fig. 4.2 Wong is pushed to the edges of the frame in *Avengers: Infinity War* (2018) as all nonwhite characters tend to be in the genre.

always portrayed by white, non-Hispanic actors—in the case of *Ghost Rider* (2007) and *Ghost Rider: Spirit of Vengeance* (2012) they are cursed . . . to be played by Nicolas Cage. A critical study conducted by Anhar Karim for *Forbes* in 2018 concluded that only 4 percent of the actors across the MCU are Hispanic—Benicio Del Toro's Collector and Maximiliano Hernández's Jasper Sitwell—and not a single major character is of Hispanic origin.[6]

There is no simple solution to these complicated issues of representation, especially in the case of multinational corporations resistant to change until it becomes profitable for them. However, the recent box office success of films like *Crazy Rich Asians* (2018), *Black Panther* (2018), and, to a lesser extent, *Overboard* (2018) combined with a greater awareness might lead one to be cautiously optimistic for the future.

Case Study: Hancock

> I apologize to the people of Los Angeles. My behavior has been improper, and I accept the consequences. I ask my fellow Angelenos for their patience and understanding. Life here can be difficult for me. After all, I am the only one of my kind. During my incarceration, I will be participating in alcohol and anger-management treatment. You deserve better from me. I can be better. I will be better.
>
> —Hancock in *Hancock* (2008)

> Over the last three decades there have been very little overt representations of the Black experience [in the superhero genre], though there have been several black superheroes, including Spawn and Black Panther, among numerous others. Comics dealing with issues specific to the African American experience, such as racial profiling, discrimination, integration, etc. have been scarce, perhaps because these realities are swept under a rug in order to avoid state responsibility for them.
>
> —Adilifu Nama, *Super Black:*
> *American Pop Culture and Black Superheroes* (2011)

Peter Berg's *Hancock*, starring Will Smith as the eponymous superhero, is an important film in the superhero genre for a number of reasons. As we have established, superhero films with black leads are incredibly rare, but this one, released in the same year that Barack Obama defeated John McCain to become the forty-fourth president of the United States, was a huge commercial success, the fourth highest-earning film in 2008 around the globe ($624 million), surpassing the box office of *Iron Man* ($585 million) and in doing so cementing Will Smith's reputation as one of the biggest film stars in the world in the second decade of his career. Returning to *Hancock* more than ten years after its initial release proves thought-provoking; while audiences flocked to see it at the time, critics and writers have been divided as to whether it should be applauded for its originality (as a rare superhero film not based on an established character) and African American lead or deplored for perpetuating racist stereotypes and trading in the casual yet explicit homophobia that had characterized American cinema for decades.[7]

Jeffrey A. Brown in *The Modern Superhero in Film and Television: Popular Genre and Culture* (2016) contends that "the implication of the narrative becomes that a superpowered black man is dangerous, criminally irresponsible with power, and generally reviled by the community until a white man teaches him acceptable behaviour and social responsibility."[8] The stereotypes that Brown observes as central to Hancock's characteriza-tion are evident even in the film's opening moments when he is introduced as drunk, irresponsible, antisocial, and immature: he flies when inebri-ated, touches one woman inappropriately, and informs another, "I been drinking, bitch!" The homophobic humor starts in the same scene, with Hancock suggesting that the Asian bank robbers he apprehends are gay and then threatening to insert their heads up each other's butts (a joke that becomes a repeating motif for the film); he later dismisses all comic book heroes as "homos." Hancock's antisocial actions, the drinking and the inappropriate behavior to women, are challenged later in the film, but his homophobia is not, and when he says to a child, "Never let them turn *that* one," indicating the child's bottom, it appears evident that the film is asking us to laugh with him rather than at him.

Ray (Jason Bateman), a white middle-class public relations consult-ant whom Hancock saves, offers the superhero some help with his image problem in the city, where some worship him and others are critical of his heavy-handed approach. Ray offers an insight into what he believes moti-vates Hancock's actions: "I think deep down you want people's accept-ance, come on now; you save people's lives and they reject you, so you reject them back." With Ray's help over the course of the film Hancock is rehabilitated into society and what the film regards as appropriate behavior for a superhero, that is, treating the public and law enforcement with an appropriate level of respect, not causing huge amounts of destruction in and around Los Angeles, and agreeing to serve prison time for his own transgressions of the law. It was this transition and how it appears to be racially coded that struck some writers as problematic; Erica Chito Childs calls Hancock a "deviant superhero."[9] Others challenged this interpretation of the film. Marc DiPaolo argues that "the message of the second half of the film repudiates the message of the first half of the film, underscoring the feeling that many viewers had that the film turns on a dime tonally and thematically at that point. In the second half of the film, it is not Hancock in particular or black men in general, who emerge as the real reason for racial strife in America, but intolerant white Americans."[10]

Hancock is effectively a black Superman, with almost all of the same powers but apparently none of the vulnerabilities. The film's biggest twist is that Ray's wife, Mary (Charlize Theron), is also a superhero and that she and Hancock are always drawn to each other through the millennia, with the unfortunate consequence that if they are together then they lose their immortal status. What they both actually *are* remains unconfirmed by the

Fig. 4.3 Will Smith's Hancock is compelled to negotiate his identity in *Hancock* (2008) in terms that appear to frame his ethnicity in coded ways.

Fig. 4.4 Critics and audiences have disagreed how far *Hancock* perpetuates racial stereotypes.

film, but Mary tells us that "gods, angels, different cultures call us different names, now all of a sudden its *superheroes*." Ray provides Hancock with new clothes more befitting a hero and gives him a purpose, which O'Brien contends "permits its black superhero to function productively only after retraining and indoctrination as a white-regulated team player."[11] As with *Wonder Woman* and *Captain Marvel*, a substantial textual and extratextual burden is placed upon *Hancock* as a rare superhero film featuring a black protagonist not placed on films from the genre that are not regarded as being important from either the perspective of gender or ethnicity. The likes of Iron Man, Spider-Man, and Batman are not considered as representative of their gender or ethnicity, but given the lack of representation of minorities this is often the case for films that feature female or black superheroes. Whether this level of scrutiny for a single film is appropriate is up to audiences to decide, but Jeffrey Brown's is an interpretation of the film that was shared by many: that "the racial dynamics imply that part of this maturation process involves rejecting stereotypically black traits and assimilating to dominant standards and expectations. To put it bluntly: to be a real hero: Hancock needs to be less black."[12]

Case Study: Black Panther

> You know, where I'm from . . . when black folks started revolutions,
> they never had the firepower . . . or the resources to fight their
> oppressors. Where was Wakanda? Hmm? Yeah, all that ends today.
> We got spies embedded in every nation on Earth. Already in place.
> I know how colonizers think. So we're gonna use their own strat-
> egy against 'em. We're gonna send vibranium weapons out to our
> War Dogs. They'll arm oppressed people all over the world . . . so
> they can finally rise up and kill those in power. And their children.
> And anyone else who takes their side. It's time they know the truth
> about us!
>   —N'Jadaka/Eric Stevens/Killmonger in *Black Panther*

> *Black Panther* is a defining moment for Black America.
>   —Carvell Wallace, *New York Times Magazine*

It is hard to know quite where to begin with a film as widely discussed
as *Black Panther*, released in February 2018 as the eighteenth film in the
MCU. Without a doubt there are few popular culture texts in the last decade
that have had as powerful a cultural impact as Ryan Coogler's film, only his
third after *Fruitvale Station* (2013) and *Creed* (2015). If one were looking
to find an example of the superhero film's cultural relevance one could
do no better than *Black Panther* which saw itself described through 2018
as "a defining moment for Black America," a "watershed," a "milestone,"
and even "for film what Barack Obama was for the presidency."[13] We recall
that one of Martin Scorsese's criticisms of the genre was that it was not
"the cinema of human beings trying to convey emotional, psychological
experiences to another human being";[14] however, the responses to *Black
Panther* testify to how much it came to mean to those who identified
with its characters or found themselves profoundly moved by the relevance of its narrative, even if it was *just* a superhero film. *Black Panther*
was eagerly anticipated by many, but no one could have anticipated its
financial success or the social and cultural significance it acquired. On
its way to earning a remarkable $1.3 billion dollars around the globe it
broke several records and achieved many "firsts" and "bests": the biggest
February domestic box office opening of all time ($202 million), the first

film since *Avatar* (2009) to spend five weeks at number one (February 16 to March 18), becoming the most preticket sales of any film not in the Star Wars franchise (1977–), the largest opening-weekend box office for a black director in film history, and, perhaps most important, the highest grossing superhero film in the United States ($700 million).

What could it have been about *a superhero film* that prompted such reactions? The paucity of black superheroes before it certainly lent it a lot of cultural baggage and expectation, as did the all black cast and the vividly realized Afrofuturist utopia of Wakanda, a rare positive portrayal of Africa on American screens. Central to the film's aesthetic and its narrative is its Afrofuturism, a neologism coined by Mark Derry in 1994, is defined by Ytasha Womack in *Afrofuturism: The World of Black Sci-Fi and Fantasy Culture* as "an intersection of imagination, technology, the future, and liberation" that reformulates "culture and notions of blackness for today and the future" by combining "elements of science fiction, historical fiction, speculative fiction, fantasy, Afrocentricity, and magic realism with non-Western beliefs."[15]

The film follows the empathetic T'Challa, who had been introduced two years before in *Captain America: Civil War*, as he comes to terms with his father's death in his journey toward becoming the king of Wakanda. When he learns that his father once killed his own brother, T'Challa's uncle, in the United States, leaving a young child behind, he is forced to recognize that his father may not have been as perfect as he had believed

Fig. 4.5 The vast majority of the characters in *Black Panther* (2018) are African American or African.

and that Wakanda's millennia-old policy of isolationism might need to be reconsidered. The abandoned child grows up to be an adult played with a brooding intensity by Michael B. Jordan and is given three names in the course of the film emblematic of the crisis of identity he experiences. The Wakandan name given to him by his father, Prince N'Jobu (Sterling K. Brown), is N'Jadaka, which is the name he seems to identify with. But his American name is Erik Stevens, and the nickname he is given during his time in the American military, both the Navy SEALs and the JSOC (Joint Special Operations Command), for his talent and propensity for violence, is Killmonger. The character has been described as the best villain in the Marvel Cinematic Universe, as "the most complex villain in the post-*Dark Knight* cycle of superhero blockbusters," and, by Slavoj Žižek, as "the film's true hero."[16]

The film's characters, themes, and spaces seemed to speak to the real-life fears, anxieties, hopes, and dreams of American (and global) audiences concerning identity, borders, belonging, and geopolitical accountability, which chimed particularly for African American audiences in the wake of Trump's contentious election victory in 2016. Manohla Dargis at the *New York Times* writes, "In its emphasis on black imagination, creation and liberation, the movie becomes an emblem of a past that was denied and a future that feels very present." And Tim Grierson at *Screen International* described a film "rooted in a desire to speak meaningfully about racism, global culture clashes, and the tension between hiding behind one's borders and helping outsiders in need."[17]

Aside from the importance of its representation of ethnicity, the film was able to transcend aspects of the genre that have historically opened the superhero film to criticism. While many of its characters do have superpowers and they are fighting for the throne of a fictional African country, the film is rooted in a sense of emotion and character development that many were able to identify with. Rather than the kinetic scenes of action and spectacle the sense is known for, it was *Black Panther*'s challenge to stereotypical representations of Africans in American film, remarkable cast of dynamic female characters, and exploration of themes related to contemporary African and African American experiences that resonated with many people all over the world, revealing the ability of the genre to make meaningful contributions to real-world discourse. The film explores and represents personal and cultural traumas across

Fig. 4.6 At the center of *Black Panther* are the two vivid and dynamic characterizations of T'Challa and N'Jadaka/Erik "Killmonger" Stevens.

generations of African Americans deprived of connections to their ancestral homelands in Africa; the weight of the past on the African continent as reflected in diverse schools of inquiry like decolonial ethics and postcolonialism; and the shifting coordinates of black masculinity in contemporary United States. Whether its intricacies are apparent to the majority of the film's audiences is impossible to know; however, *Black Panther* showed that the superhero film could transcend the genre in a range of ways that cemented its significance and relevance.

5   THE GLOBAL CONTEMPORARY SUPERHERO FILM

Those with real power aren't people like us. They were born to win.
Do you know what they can do? Do you think they can fire energy
waves or something? No. They have power over this country. . . .
The country itself is their power. Everyone else, including you and
me, are just slaves of society. Why can't you accept it? Know your
place. . . .

Hong Sang-moo in *Psychokinesis* (2018)

Many national cultures have created (or re-imagined) superheroic
figures, and the world of superheroes now contains many icons
whose histories borrow from local folklore, myths and legends.
Consequently, the superhero needs to be reconsidered, to be seen
as part of global and local culture, and examined for rich meanings
that such divergent origins and reworkings can create.

—Rayna Denison, Rachel Mizsei-Ward, and Derek Johnston,
Superheroes on World Screens (2015)

The vast majority of the films explored in this book have been those
produced by the American film industry, regarded as examples of both
American cinema's industrial practices and its cultural narratives, but at
the same time they should also be understood as global texts in a variety
of ways. While the films still remain resolutely American, with almost all

of their characters American and being predominantly set in the United States, they exhibit a much greater awareness of the demands of global audiences than ever before, a market which now makes considerably more money for American blockbusters than the domestic U.S. market. This becomes manifested in the tendency to move the characters around the world more than ever happened before the genre's renaissance. In the "original" Batman film franchise (1989–97) scenes outside the United States are almost nonexistent, but the more recent addition to the series, *Batman v Superman: Dawn of Justice*, has sequences in India, Russia, Tonga, Afghanistan, and a fictional African country, Nairomi. In the same way entrants to the Marvel Cinematic Universe routinely have adventures all over the globe in ways which serve their narrative and the international box office, thus sojourns to South Korea like those featured in *Avengers: Age of Ultron* and *Black Panther* garner considerable tax incentives for the production at the same time as appealing to South Korean audiences. Similarly, the casting of international performers, as in the case of the Chinese Wang Xueqi and Fan Bingbing in *Iron Man 3*, appeals in the same way and even resulted in a different cut of the film specifically to cater to Chinese markets. To return to the Batman franchise, *Batman* made most of its money domestically, as did *Batman Returns* and *Batman Forever*, with only *Batman & Robin* making marginally more abroad than at home in 1997. However, of the six superhero films in the top ten global box office in 2018 only *Black Panther* made more in the United States than it did abroad, one of just three films in the top twenty to do so (the others were *Dr Seuss' The Grinch* and *A Star Is Born*). For those six superhero films, an average of 61.6 percent of their total income came from the international box office, with *Aquaman* and *Venom*'s international takes reaching 71.8 and 75 percent, respectively. Columbia Pictures and Sony would no doubt have been disappointed by *Venom*'s U.S. box office total of $213.5 million, but when this is added to the $642 million it earned in international markets the film surprisingly ended up as the sixth biggest box office success of the year.

As interesting as the increasingly global dimensions of Hollywood film productions are, this chapter is about superhero films made outside of the United States, even though the influences of American articulations of the genre remain prominent. I choose to primarily use the word *global* rather than *foreign* as the latter is suggestive of a binary between American and Other that has become increasingly outdated in what we now refer to as the global age. In this context *foreign* also reads as pejorative rather than just descriptive, suggestive of America as the home of cinema with everything else a distant Other. It hardly seems necessary to mention that American films are foreign to every other country in the world, and as Elizabeth Ezra and Terry Rowden wrote in *Transnational Cinema: The Film Reader* (2006) it is also "important to recognize the impossibility of maintaining a strict dichotomy between Hollywood cinema and its 'others.' "[1]

Therefore, there are a tapestry of superhero films from around the globe of varying quality, from Spain's *Superlópez* (2018), India's Krrish series (2003–), Finland's *Rendel* (2017), Russia's *Guardians* (2017), Denmark's Antboy series (2013–), Britain's *SuperBob* (2015), South Korea's *Psychokinesis* (2018), Japan's *Casshern* (2004), Thailand's *Mercury Man* (2006), France's *Vincent Has No Scales* (2014), Italy's *They Call Me Jeeg* (2015), and many others. These films are worthy of consideration for a variety of reasons, but they tend to be ignored outside of their own cultures and sometimes even inside them. Indeed, the vast majority of them are not afforded a cinema release beyond their own domestic markets, and very few of them have even been heard of by audiences outside. This lack of exposure is not an indication of poor quality, but as a direct result of being seen less they also are discussed and written about less by a body of literature that often assumes that the superhero film begins and ends with American contributions to the genre. Thus given its title it might be expected that Jeffrey Brown's *The Modern Superhero in Film and Television: Popular Genre and American Culture* does not turn its attention to global superhero films, but what should we make of the fact that in *The 21st Century Superhero: Essays on Gender, Genre, and Globalization in Film, Gender, and the Superhero Narrative* (2011), *The Superhero Reader* (2013), and *The Mythology of the Superhero* (2016) there is not a single chapter or extended analysis of a superhero film from outside of the United States? This is not to criticize these works, which have each made a significant contribution to studies of the genre, but just to emphasize how American culture has defined what a superhero film, and indeed what a superhero, is considered to be.

Global superhero films operate in a challenging arena in a number of ways as they are likely to be directly compared to those made by the American film industry by audiences and as one of the primary pleasures of the genre lies in the spectacular images and action sequences they contain, global productions are often found wanting as a result of their budgetary constraints, as no film industry outside the United States can afford the capital required to put a film like *Avengers: Infinity War* on the screen, with its budget of $356 million, *Batman v Superman* at $250 million, *Green Lantern* at $200 million, *The Dark Knight* at $185 million, *Wonder Woman* at $149 million, *X-Men: First Class* at $160 million, *Logan* at $97 million, *Hellboy* (2019) at $66 million, or even *Deadpool* at $58 million. These figures do not even take into account marketing and publicity, which can sometimes double the original production budget. Comparatively, one of our case studies in this chapter is the British superhero film *SuperBob* which cost £1 million to make, a figure that Phil de Semlyen joked "probably wouldn't cover the *Avengers*' catering."[2] However, there is no *probably* about it according to reports about how expensive catering on modern blockbusters has become. One million dollars was how much each of the costumes for the eponymous hero of *Shazam!* cost to make according to director David F. Sandberg, and they made not one, but ten of them![3] Yet even the modest budget of *SuperBob* exceeds that of every installment in the Malaysian superhero franchise featuring the character known as Cicak-Man (*cicak* is the Malay word for lizard): *Cicak-Man* (2006) was made for less than half a million dollars, and *Cicak-Man 2: Planet Hitam* (2008) and *Cicak-Man 3* (2015) each cost around $750,000. These much smaller budgets often result in films that appear cheap or amateurish and therefore unappealing to many Western audiences not used to the styles, rhythms, and idiosyncrasies of other national cinemas.

Another factor preventing these global superhero films from being seen more widely is the reluctance of English-speaking countries to embrace subtitled films. While there are rare breakthrough examples (see *Crouching Tiger, Hidden Dragon* [2000], *Amélie* [2001], and *Pan's Labyrinth* [2006]), studies suggest that mainstream American audiences overwhelmingly prefer films in English and even actively avoid foreign films.[4] Therefore, the Cicak-Man franchise, the first Malaysian superhero films, had very little chance to ever be seen by audiences outside of its own country and never received a cinema release in the United States or the UK, with only limited availability on DVD. They are categorically Malaysian in the way they are constructed but profoundly influenced by American permutations of the superhero genre, with a story decidedly reminiscent of Stan Lee's Spider-Man. The first two films feature the clumsy underachiever

Hairi (Saiful Apek), a laboratory assistant who accidentally acquires the powers of a lizard after being infected by a virus in the lab he works in, and the third focuses on his successor, Man (Zizan Razak), an unemployed superhero fanatic who inherits the mantle of Cicak-Man after finding a superhero serum inside a statue of his hero. Both iterations of Cicak-Man adhere closely to Peter Coogan's powers, identity, and mission template: their heroic abilities are what one would expect from a lizard as opposed to a spider (strength, climbing walls, enhanced agility and a protruding tongue); their identity is a closely guarded secret; and their suit is a bit too heavily influenced by Daredevil. Their mission is to protect innocent civilians who reside in the futuristic and densely populated Metrofulus, which in the first two films is terrorized by the theatrical supervillain Professor Klon (a combination of the Joker and the Riddler) and his absurdly coiffed henchmen, the Ginger Boys.

The franchise would undoubtedly struggle to resonate with Western audiences because of its rudimentary CGI (especially in the first two films), limited production values, melodramatic performances, and hysterically exaggerated product placement that puts even the most egregious Hollywood films to shame. This combined leads to the first two films at times being reminiscent of 1990s Saturday morning children's television shows like *Mighty Morphin Power Rangers* (Fox, 1993–1996), but this did not stop *Cicak-Man* breaking the opening-day record for a Malaysian film by grossing RM350,000 in its domestic market.[5] By the release of the third and best film in the franchise, *Cicak-Man 3* in 2015, the Western superhero renaissance had become a more prominent influence, and the quirkiness of the first two installments is diluted by a concerted attempt to ground the story and characters in a way that echoes contemporary American films from the genre. When violent gangs take over Metrofulus after the disappearance of Cicak-Man, a harder-edged and brutal superhero, Superbro, promises to return law and order to the streets with his zero-tolerance brand of justice. It is tempting to connect aspects of this narrative to the authoritarian politics of late twentieth-century and early twenty-first-century Malaysian culture much as American superhero films in this period have come to be defined by the social and political backdrop of the War on Terror. Certainly, the film features an unpalatable vein of homophobic humor from its opening scenes to its last, an unfortunate reflection of

Malaysia's regressive state, where homosexuality is illegal and there are no antidiscrimination laws concerning sexual identity.[6]

The Cicak-Man franchise also "suffers," as do many global superhero films, in the sense that its cultural references are very particular to Malaysia and would not be understandable to those outside, in this case foreign audiences, with the term here including those from America and the UK, something that American superhero films do not experience given the absolute primacy of American popular culture around the world. Thus there is a good chance that audiences from Albania to Zimbabwe might understand who Tony Stark is referring to when he calls Corvus Glaive "Squidward" in *Avengers: Infinity War*, from the long-running children's television show *SpongeBob SquarePants* (Nickelodeon, 1999–) or who Kevin Bacon is when Star-Lord talks about him in *Guardians of the Galaxy* or even Nick Fury's reference to "flying monkeys" from *The Wizard of Oz* (1939) in *The Avengers*. However, it is highly unlikely that those outside Malaysia would know that a question about Professor Klon's clones being "Original or Spicy?" is a reference to the largest fast-food brand in Malaysia or that a joke about their being "ori" concerns the Malaysian government's ongoing battle to prevent internet piracy.[7]

This brief overview of the Malaysian Cicak-Man franchise highlights some of the problems confronting not just the global superhero film but also many national film industries around the world, faced with audiences who overwhelmingly tend to prefer American films to those produced in their own countries. In 2015, the year of the release of *Cicak-Man 3*, only a single non-Hollywood film topped the Malaysian box office, the Chinese action-comedy *The Man from Macau II* (2015). In the Philippines, the location of *Captain Barbell* discussed below, at the time of writing only three of the highest grossing films of all time are indigenously produced, with twelve of the top nineteen being American superhero films. Some countries have less of a problem with this, for example, Turkey, where seven of the top ten films in 2017 were Turkish (see also China, India, and Japan). In Britain, where this monograph was written, the BFI (British Film Institute) states that six of the top ten films at the box office should be considered British, but that is only if one considers *Star Wars: The Force Awakens* and *Avengers: Endgame* British, which somewhat incredibly the BFI does, with its tortuous logic also counting *Justice League* (2018), *Doctor Strange* (2017),

Wonder Woman (2017), *Avengers: Age of Ultron* (2015), and *Ant-Man* (2015) as British films.

Another significant problem for global superhero films is that there appears to be a widely held opinion that those which appear from international film industries are cheap "knock-offs" of superior American "original" versions of the genre. This is something comprehensively challenged by Iain Robert Smith in *The Hollywood Meme: Transnational Adaptations in World Cinema* in his analysis of the Turkish film industry in particular and its comparatively lax copyright laws, with infamous examples like *3 Giant Men* (*3 Dev Adam*) a 1973 film that features Captain America, Spider-Man, and a Mexican superhero and wrestler, with Spider-Man as the villain. Smith's work asks us to question the relationship between the United States and global cinema, suggesting it should be "read in terms of cultural exchange and transnational media flow . . . not be perceived simply as American culture dominating over and homogenizing other cultures" but a "process through which cultures meet and interact."[8]

The global superhero film instead should be understood as manifestations of international cinematic and industrial practices but also unique national identities and monomyths, at the same time impacted upon and influenced in complicated ways by the domination of the superhero form by the American cultural industries. Take, for example, two films heavily inspired by the character of Superman (and in particular Donner's *Superman*): *Captain Barbell* (2003) from the Philippines and *Superlópez* (2018) from Spain. *Captain Barbell* appears brazenly derivative on the surface, drawing explicitly from the likes of Superman and Shazam, yet this belies the character's own significant history in the Philippines since his creation by Mars Ravelo and Jim Fernandez, his first appearance in *Pinoy Komiks* no. 5 (May 23, 1963) and also the complicated relationship between the United States and the Philippines, which has been described as both imperial and neocolonial. Nick Cullather suggests that the Philippines is "a country that surrendered its identity to the cultural, economic, and military domination of the United States" in the twentieth century.[9]

Captain Barbell's story, which is faithfully adapted from the comics into the 2003 film, centers on the kind-hearted but naive Enteng (Ogie Alcasid), who finds a magic barbell in the gym where he works that when lifted with the cry of "Captain Barbell!" results in his being transformed into the eponymous superhero. We are given ample demonstration of Enteng's sincerity and goodness before he becomes Captain Barbell—how he looks after his beloved adoptive mother, gives her all his salary, and refuses to trouble her when he needs new shoes, telling her, "Don't worry mother, it's in fashion"—which echoes Steve Rogers before he received the Super Soldier serum. Enteng, too, is bullied, but unlike Cap he refuses to fight back against those who beat and taunt him and declines the advances of a girl he deems too forward. When Eteng makes the transition to Captain Barbell he is played by a different actor (as in the case of *Shazam!*), but he is also a *different person*, with some awareness of his original personality, which sometimes comes through at key moments in the film.

Captain Barbell has no time for the veristic turn taken by many recent American superhero films, featuring caricatured villains like Lagablab, the fire-breathing man, and Dagampat, the poison-spitting rat man. But the film also makes it clear that the Philippines in which it is set is a dangerous place that requires figures like Captain Barbell to stand up for the innocent by transgressing the law, as we see so often in American superhero films. At one point Captain Barbell tells a girl after saving her from a group of thugs who seem bent on sexually abusing her, "Next time you be careful . . . these are dangerous times!" Later the news reports, "A man took a woman hostage and the suspect seems to be under the influence of drugs", which prompts Enteng's mother to remark, "The Philippines is really getting bad," a comment that has led some to argue that the film is one of many from Filipino popular cinema that evokes the authoritarian tendencies the country has displayed in recent decades.[10] Despite the melodrama, and unlike many of his American counterparts, Captain Barbell does fail in one of his missions, and a boy dies in a fire because Barbell selfishly considered his own needs and arrived too late, something that has never happened to Iron Man, Captain America, or Superman in any of their films, with their veneer of vulnerability only a superficial patina. Captain Barbell chastises himself with the words "I *have to* sacrifice my own personal happiness for those who need Captain Barbell!" but the lines seem self-consciously designed to reach out beyond the frames to young audiences throughout the Philippines, telling them to remain chaste, stay away from drugs, and respect their elders.

In contrast, *Superlópez* is a much more parodic retelling of the Superman story, transplanting it to modern day Spain, but it too is drawn from a popular series of comics first created in 1973, resulting in a film that is as inherently Spanish as *Captain Barbell* is Filipino. Its main character is Juan López, a mild-mannered office worker who happens to be an alien from the planet Chitón, saved by his biological parents who sent him away in a spaceship which leads to him being discovered and adopted by simple Spanish farmers. Juan tries to live a normal life and hide his superhero powers, but it becomes impossible when he is discovered by another Chitónian, Ágata Müller, who is bent on destroying him and taking over the world. His prospective girlfriend, not Lois Lane but Luisa Lanas, is initially incredulous that a superhero might come from Spain, saying, "Some things don't fit: superheroes and Spanish? No!" and even asks, "Who's the villain, punctuality?" In the end, Juan embraces his powers and reconciles himself to being both Superlópez and Juan, just as Clarke Kent has attempted to do since 1939. Juan also wears a large S on a suit made for him by his mother, who says with tongue firmly in cheek, "I *copied* this from the Supermen movies." The film concludes with news reports that echo criticisms of the genre in a humorous way: "This country has had *real* superheroes, Don Pelayo, El Cid. We don't deserve some guy flying around in a leotard" and "I think this superhero is a smokescreen . . . so we don't talk about *what really matters!*"

Another intriguing example of a global superhero film which departs from some of the parameters established by American incarnations of the form is *Psychokinesis* (2018), made in South Korea, financed by Netflix, and directed by Yeon Sang-ho, who had gained commercial and critical acclaim

Fig. 5.1 Does the Spanish superhero film *Superlópez* (2018) pay homage to American classics of the genre or steal from them?

for his propulsive zombie film *Train to Busan* (2016). *Psychokinesis* was widely touted as South Korea's first superhero film and is both profoundly influenced by American entrants to the genre and also immersed in its own culture as we have seen in the case of *Cicak-Man, Captain Barbell,* and *Superlópez.* Described by Richard Gray as "a fresh take on a superhero origin story that combines sharp social commentary, comedy, and some impressively scaled action sequences,"[11] it deviates from the codes and conventions of the genre in ways both large and small. It is one of the rare superhero films not to be named after its main character, and it also refuses to give its hero a costume or a heroic identity, but more importantly, instead of the world being at stake it revolves around a local community of shop owners who have lost faith in the system ("The law won't help us"; "The cops won't even bother coming here anyway"; "Everyone sides with money!") and how they fight back against a large corporation represented by Director Hong, who seeks to evict them and make millions by developing the land on which their businesses stand. The protagonist, Seok-heon, receives his powers after a meteor strike infects the water of

Fig. 5.2 *Psychokinesis* (2018), South Korea's first superhero film, deviates from the codes and conventions of the genre in several compelling ways.

a local nature park, and the film follows him as he seeks to reestablish a relationship with his estranged daughter, Ru Mi, one of those threatened with relocation and later violence by Hong's corporation. Seok-heon is one of the least likely superheroes ever given the title: middle-aged, selfish, and lazy, with a generous paunch and an ambiguous relationship with the law. He initially tries to financially profit from his new powers by becoming a magician. After Ru Mi's mother is killed in a fracas with the corporation's hired muscle he finds himself able to make a difference and earn back his daughter's respect, articulating this clearly: "Maybe I have been given this ability so I can be a good dad for a change?" Like fathers Scott Lang in *Ant-Man* ("No, I'm serious, man. I'm not going back. I got a daughter to take care of") and Melvin (Stephen Dorf) in *American Hero* (2017) ("I'm gonna do whatever it takes, no more weed, pills, I'm even thinking about stopping jerking off!") he forgoes crime to reconnect with his child.

However, by highlighting real social problems *Psychokinesis* ties the superhero film to a socially progressive narrative in ways rarely touched upon by the genre, a tendency for which we have seen it justifiably criticized.[12] When Seok-heon is imprisoned and Hong offers him a chance to join the corporation, he seems genuinely torn between his two choices but ultimately chooses to side with his daughter, to the disbelief of the director, who would have him work for her company—just as many writers have suggested that characters like Captain America, Iron Man, and Superman do for the state in American superhero films. Yet *Psychokinesis* cannot veer too far from the formula of a superhero film, and as Coogan asserts, "The mission convention is essential to the superhero genre because someone who does not act selflessly to aid others in times of need is not heroic and therefore not a hero."[13] Seok-heon sides with his daughter's group in an elaborate and impressively staged final battle against the forces of the corporation and even the South Korean police. American superheroes rarely fight directly against the state, usually opposing individuals or groups outside the state apparatus or sometimes those who have infiltrated it. In another rare occurrence the hero is not victorious at the end of *Psychokinesis*. Seok-heon and the shopkeepers lose the final battle, and he is sent to prison. The film ends with a coda that reveals that the corporation never developed on the land it was willing to kill for and shows Seok-heon released from prison and invited back into his daughter's life after having earned her trust.

The global superhero film offers compelling engagements with the genre, with similarities and differences to American forms frequently offering an insight into its codes and conventions and also its possibilities and limitations, steeped as they are in their own social and political contexts, but blended with American formulations of the genre. These complicated interactions provide us with an embodiment of the relationship between the dominance of the American culture industries and films made by other national cinemas which is one of the hallmarks of film production in the global age.

Case Study: SuperBob

> He should be used in the right way. You people are sitting on the greatest discovery of this century, and you are squandering it!
> —Senator Jackson in *SuperBob* (2015)

> The idea of the British superhero is often considered to be a contradiction in terms. Superheroes belong to America. They soar between the skyscrapers of the great American cities, both real and imagined, from New York to Metropolis, Chicago to Gotham. They represent the ideals of "truth, Justice, and the American way." Moreover, while superheroes are popular all over the world, nowhere is the association between the genre and the comics medium as close it is in America.
> —Chris Murray, *The British Superhero* (2017)

Such has been the hold of American conceptions of the superhero genre that Chris Murray's comment, which provides an epigraph to this section might be applied to almost any country that produces a superhero film, not just the example of Great Britain that he uses. Does even the term "superhero" conjure up American characters and landscapes just as much as that other quintessentially American genre or the Western? What might a British superhero look like on the screen? Who would they be and what would they do? It is not as if Britain lacks a rich vein of heroic mythology to tap into, through the likes of Robin Hood, Saint George, and King Arthur and his knights of the Round Table. In previous decades comic book superheroes like Union Jack (1976), Captain Britain (1976), and Beefeater

(1989), with an exaggerated sense of Britishness evident even in their names, have been American interpretations of British superheroes. These characters are part of a tradition of the most powerful American comic book companies defining the identity of superheroes from other countries: the Australian Captain Boomerang (1960), the Puerto Rican White Tiger (1975), the Russian Colossus (1975), the Irish Shamrock (1982), the French Nightrunner (2011), the South Korean White Fox (2015), and most recently the Filipino Wave (2019).

SuperBob is an attempt to answer the question, as the film's director, Jon Drever, stated, "What's important to me is that this film is not a pastiche or a spoof; this is what Brett [Goldstein] and I think a British superhero would be like. One of the central conceits is 'what would [it] be like for a superhero [who] actually existed and what if he was British?' "[14] Adapted from their 2009 short film into a feature, SuperBob, a.k.a. Bob Kenner (Brett Goldstein), is a mild-mannered postman who makes an interesting addition to this roster as a rare example of an actual British superhero.[15] The film did not even receive a cinema release in the UK and is a low-budget comedy which features little of the excesses we have come to expect from American superhero films like *Avengers: Age of Ultron* and

Fig. 5.3 The question "What might a British superhero look like?" is answered in *SuperBob* (2015).

Ant-Man, released in the same year. Bob gets his powers when he is accidentally struck by a meteorite in Peckham, south London, which gives him abilities very similar to those of Superman. Instead of the relative freedom one might expect that this affords him, Bob is quickly taken control of by representatives of the British government and the Ministry of Defence in the form of Theresa (Catherine Tate). Rather than the Sokovia Accords, the Keene Act, or the Mutant Registration Act, this emerges in the form of extensive and perhaps very British conceptions of bureaucracy, which involve forms being filled in *before* and *after* every rescue.

SuperBob adopts the mockumentary style that became popular in the wake of *The Office* (BBC, 2001–3) and *Borat* (2006) but can be traced back to *This Is Spinal Tap* (1984).[16] The camera crew that follows the characters in *SuperBob* is explained within the diegesis as being done in an effort to produce a documentary film which will humanize Bob for the public. *SuperBob* is a comedy, "the most popular of all genres in British cinema,"[17] and the film appears somewhat frivolous, but it is at the same time a genre which provides a site "where social commentary, cultural critique, and the crisis of representation collide, where humour—whether in the form of blatant laughter or simply rueful shakes of the head—meets reflection."[18] The humor in *SuperBob* targets Bob's rather mundane life as he is interviewed by Jon, the film's actual director Jon Drever, which is far removed from the glamorous hedonism of Iron Man or the spectacularly noble heroics of Superman. Instead, Bob is an everyday and rather dull guy who considers himself a civil servant rather than a superhero. He has a United Nations sanctioned day off every Tuesday, a security guard ("a union thing"), is not considered a "real" superhero by many (someone calls his superhero name "a bit arrogant"), and he is initially criticized by those in his local community, one of whom manipulates him to take her place in the queue for the post office, something it is hard to imagine Batman or Rorshach doing. It would also be hard to imagine any other hero being introduced as Bob is, by his Colombian cleaner Dorris (Natalia Tena), whom Bob realizes he is in love with, asking him on camera if he has evacuated his bowels that morning. In this sense he is one of the genre's most down-to-earth characters, as one newsreader remarks "a superhero for the *real* world," and *SuperBob* joins other comedic superhero films, such as *Special* (2006), *Defendor* (2009), and *Super* (2010), that have attempted something similar. What makes *SuperBob* different even from these films is its rejection of some of the genre's essential tenets, like the demand for violent altercations; as the film contains absolutely no fights at all and Bob does not display any of the qualities of the overtly masculinized characters that populate the genre; quite the opposite, he is gentle, kind, self-effacing, and the very model of a "new man." The film does not even provide Bob with an antagonist; the closest it comes to this is the American senator Jackson, who is jealous of the fact that Britain has the only superhero in the world and demands that he be "better" used, that is, to support American interests around the globe, informing Bob, "There's gonna be a lot of money in it for ya!" The control that the state demands over him leads to a mild personality crisis for Bob, resulting in him seeking more autonomy over his life. This comes to a head when he dares to try rescue the victim of a car accident on his day off, which by law he is not allowed to do, only to see the woman die anyway, and when he learns that Theresa has sent Dorris back to Colombia. She tells him he "can't be with anyone from Colombia . . . it's really not

Fig. 5.4 Bob is manipulated by those around him and forced to wear a multicolored costume representative of all the countries bidding for his services in *SuperBob*.

the right narrative," and she would prefer that he date an American girl to further the "special relationship" between England and the United States. Bob learns this at the "SuperBob summit," where it also becomes clear that his services are being loaned to other countries in exchange for preferential trade deals and he is forced to exchange his usual black leather costume for something more multicolored that will allow other countries to believe that he represents them as well as Britain. This is the final straw for Bob, and he refuses, which sees him labeled "a rogue WMD" by Jackson and criticized by his own government, leading to an offer of asylum from Ecuador, in a nod to Julian Assange's prolonged residence in the Ecuadorian embassy (2012–19). Bob returns to Peckham to tell Dorris he loves her and this time finds not criticism but support from his local community, as they rally round him in his time of trouble as one of their own. The film ends with Bob's rejection of being controlled by Britain or the United States in ways rare in the genre, announcing to the world, "I am no longer the property of Great Britain!" Like many superheroes, his story has been one about finding his identity, and he concludes his journey as Tony Stark and Spider-Man did, but in a particularly British way, "I'm not a civil servant . . . I'm SuperBob."

Case Study: Krrish

> Anyone who takes away tears and spreads happiness is Krrish . . .
> —Krrish in *Krrish 3* (2013)

> [Rakesh] Roshan's film *Krrish* (2006), the sequel to *Koi . . . Mil Gaya* [2003], extends its predecessor's portrait of hegemonic resistance and Indian identity. It accomplishes this by invoking sequelisation as a framework with which to separate more fully the cinematic codes of Bollywood from those of Hollywood, and to render distinct notions of 'Indian-ness' from Western values and identities, at the same time as the film is situated firmly in a 'global' context.
> —Carolyn Jess-Cooke, *Film Sequels: Theory and Practice from Hollywood to Bollywood* (2009)

Outside of the United States it is without a doubt the Indian film industry that has produced the most entrants to the superhero genre since its renaissance. Reaching back as early as *Mr India* (1987), Indian superhero films often draw extensively on India's own rich mythology and culture and iconic texts like the Ramayana and the Mahabharata, but at the same time they fairly explicitly borrow from American films of the genre—although not often to the extent of B. Gupta's *Superman* (1987), a film that uses *actual* shots from Donner's 1978 film. Since then Indian superhero films have been as varied as their American counterparts: the mythological drama of *Drona* (2008), the videogame-influenced *Ra.One* (2011), the comedic *A Flying Jatt* (2011), the more grounded *Bhavesh Joshi: Superhero* (2018), the heist-influenced *Prince* (2010), and the comedic *Super Singh* (2017) and *Velayudhan* (2011), each with their own distinctive connections to the country in which they were made.

The stylistic excesses of Bollywood film have traditionally been hard for Western audiences to reconcile themselves to, and outside of a few breakthrough hits like *Lagaan* (2001), *Dangal* (2016), and *Secret Superstar* (2017) the majority have failed to achieve success at the Western box office. However, when foreign audiences become accustomed to their idiosyncrasies, their codes and conventions, their extravagant dance numbers, their abrupt tonal shifts, and their sometimes egregious product placement, their pleasures are many and diverse. Unlike *Cicak-Man* or *SuperBob*, which were unable to compete financially with American superhero films, Indian superhero films like *Enthiran* (2010) and *2.0* (2018) are embraced by audiences and make more money than American films in their own domestic market. *Krrish 3* made about $50 million at the Indian box office in the same year that *Iron Man 3* made only $11.1 million and *Man of Steel* $6 million in the same region. India is a rare market where, unlike Malaysia, the UK, and most other countries, Hollywood films receive a minority share of the box office revenue, only around 10 percent per year.

The most financially successful and culturally impactful of these by far is a series of films that has defined the genre in India: the Krrish franchise, comprising *Koi . . . Mil Gaya* (2003), *Krrish* (2006), and *Krrish 3* (2013), which had the highest single-day opening in the history of the Indian box office at the time of its release. The films, directed by Rakesh Roshan and starring his son, Hrithik Roshan, one of the iconic stars of Bollywood film and widely regarded as the Bollywood Tom Cruise (he even starred in the Bollywood remake of Cruise's film *Knight and Day* [2010], called *Bang*

Bang! [2013]), have become one of the largest franchises in Indian film history, expanding beyond the cinema to television, comics, merchandising, and video games. The first in the series *Koi . . . Mil Gaya* concerns a simple but brilliant scientist, Rohit (Hrithik Roshan), who is gifted powers by an alien which are transferred to his son, Krishna, played by the same actor in the second and third installments, in films with increasingly larger budgets, more characters, more special effects, and more and more elaborate action sequences. After the apparent death of his father, Krishna is raised in the idyllic countryside by his grandmother, who is afraid that if the world learns of her grandson's powers he will be manipulated just as his father was. Yet Krishna cannot avoid his destiny, and after he meets Priya (Priyanka Chopra) he follows her to Singapore, where he becomes the masked superhero Krrish. Having promised his grandmother never to reveal his powers, he wears a broken kabuki mask that allows him to conceal his identity.

Krrish is constructed as a particularly Indian superhero who embodies and articulates Indian religious beliefs in ways far removed from the secular humanism of the MCU superheroes. Hinduism informs not only Krishna's name but also his values and what he comes to represent to those that he serves who come to revere him. He tells those he saves, who are most often women and children, that *they too* are Krrish and that "anyone who takes away tears and spreads happiness *is* Krrish," which culminates in a remarkable scene in *Krrish 3* when a statue is erected in his honor with the English inscription "Superhero of India," at its base in English quite far removed from the somber statue of Batman at the conclusion of *The Dark Knight Rises*. The film shows a large crowd assembling around the figure breaking into the song and dance number "God, Allah, Aur Bhagwan," the three gods in its title revealing the extent of the film's immersion in religion. The film's villain, Kaal (Vivek Oberoi), a mix between Professor X and Magneto, asks, "A million gods rule over India, and people have immense faith in them. Let's find out if any one of their gods can save them?" His question is answered in Krrish, who is portrayed as godlike throughout the series and whose appearance is often prefaced with lines like, "God, please help us!" However, the implication that *Krrish* and *Krrish 3* offer is not that Krrish is a deity but rather he is an instrument of god and a living embodiment of the religious faith of the Indian people.

The centrality of religion in the Krrish films is to be found in almost all Indian superhero films, unlike their American counterparts, where religion is elided completely or referred to humorously, like the line Joss Whedon scripted for Captain America in *The Avengers*, "There's only one God ma'am, and I'm pretty sure he doesn't dress like that." And in *Avengers: Infinity War*, Peter Quill/Star-Lord says, "What master do I serve? What am I supposed to say, *Jesus*?" And in *Deadpool: The Super Duper Cut* Deadpool both calls himself "merely a vessel for the lord" and later suggests he is a god. It is not a coincidence that the villains of *Krrish*, *Krrish 3*, *Ra.One*, and *A Flying Jatt* are clearly identified as atheists, as opposed to the devout superheroes they fight against. In *Ra.One* the eponymous villain (for some reason the film is named after the villain) yells, "There is no God!" but the hero G.One (Shah Rukh Khan) is shown to pray and quote from scripture. In *A Flying Jatt* the film's protagonist, Aman (Tiger Shroff), initially shrugs off his mother's complaints that he is too casual about his Sikh faith (he refuses to grow a beard and wear a turban), but after he receives powers actually from god and a khanda symbol is miraculously burned onto his muscular body, he embraces Sikhism once more.

Krrish and *Krrish 3* mount an impressive spectacle on their budgets of $6.5 million and $20 million, small by Hollywood standards though generous compared to *SuperBob*. They are more melodramatic and light-hearted than their American counterparts and contain the dancing and singing that is customary for the majority of Bollywood productions. Despite this they are not afraid to show civilians dying onscreen and even in Krrish's arms. In one sequence he carries a dying, plague-infected girl as he runs through the contaminated streets of Mumbai, a city where people are shown to be hurt and even die onscreen, leading the hero to admit to his father, "I can hear their screams and *I am helpless....*"

Just as we have seen that American films from the genre are defined and also constrained by the culture which produced them, so are those from India, as Anupama Chopra observed in a review of *Krrish 3* in the *Hindustan Times*:

> Spare a thought for the Indian superhero. Unlike his Western counterparts—Batman, Superman, Iron Man—our guy can't be dark or brooding. There is no room in his narrative for irony or angst. Not only does he have to save the world, he also has to sing and dance.

Fig. 5.5 *Krrish 3* (2013) borrows from American permutations of the genre but produces something uniquely Indian in the process.

Fig. 5.6 Despite the fantastical excesses of Bollywood's addition to the genre, *Krrish 3* has a superhero who admits he has failed those who believe in him in ways American heroes have found almost impossible to do.

He has to propagate family values, convincingly overact in thunder-
ing melodrama, defeat a villain who, like most villains in Bollywood,
laughs a lot and he must cater to and eventually seduce an audience that has grown up without a superhero comic book culture.
And he must do all this on a fraction of the budget that Hollywood
superheroes enjoy.[19]

But rather than a burden, for Indian audiences at least, this is in some
ways liberating. Krrish and other Indian superheroes resonate not despite
these cultural flourishes but because "Krrish can dance and sing, and
Spider-Man cannot, but mostly because Krrish is more rooted in our
[Indian] culture."[20]

Like many Bollywood productions the Krrish films borrow a little too
extensively from American superhero films featuring Spider-Man, Superman
and Batman, but also from American films as diverse as *First Blood* (1982),
E.T. The Extra-Terrestrial (1982), and *The Matrix* (1999) with even their
soundtracks leaning rather heavily on Alan Silvestri's score for *The Avengers*
and Hans Zimmer's for *Pirates of the Caribbean: The Curse of the Black Pearl*
(2003) for inspiration. As Sujay Kumar writes, *Krrish 3* is "a potpourri of
set-pieces and characters plucked out of every superhero film to come out
of Hollywood in the last ten years or so."[21] Whether this is homage, plagia-
rism, or what Carolyn Jess-Cooke calls "hegemonic resistance" is a matter
that the courts have sometimes had to decide.[22] But what remains are films
that are uniquely Indian in the increasingly complicated ways that art forms
are vessels of national identity in the new millennium.

CONCLUSION

"Is it me or is it getting crazier out there?": The Future of the Contemporary Superhero Film and the Genre's "Impossible Solutions for Insoluble Problems"

> Everybody wants a happy ending, right? But it doesn't always roll that way . . . God, what a world. Universe now. If you told me ten years ago that we weren't alone, let alone you know to this extent . . . I mean, I wouldn't have been surprised. But come on, you know. . . . But then again that's the hero gig. Part of the journey is the end . . .
>
> —Tony Stark in *Avengers: Endgame* (2019)

> We have this history of impossible solutions for insoluble problems . . .
>
> —Will Eisner (2005)

This book has attempted to explore and interrogate some of the parameters of the contemporary superhero film, certainly the most impactful and financially successful genre of the twenty-first century. Whereas once audiences flocked to see westerns and musicals, it is now in the superhero film that they have their cinematic fantasies fulfilled and where they find, as the cartoonist and writer Will Eisner states in the epigraph to this conclusion, "impossible solutions for insoluble problems." These insoluble problems are very much those of the real world, but the superhero film projects them through the prism of a genre which continues to provide a "mythic massage" in the words of Lawrence and Jewett, in the turbulent new millennial decades that have been defined by the traumatic events of September 11, 2001, the War on Terror, the global financial crisis, and the increasingly partisan years of Obama's second term into the Trump presidency. This might also explain why cinemagoers from Australia to Japan and Russia to Zimbabwe have flocked to see them and why, in many cases, filmmakers from those countries have made superhero films of their own.[1] Might these global audiences also have found refuge in the superhero film from their own tumultuous political climate in an era about which Arthur Fleck, a.k.a. Joker, asked, "Is it me, or is it getting crazier out there?" in *Joker* (2019). In this sense we can understand the renaissance and cultural ascendency of the superhero film in both personal and much broader cultural ways, as Ben Saunders does in *Do Gods Wear Capes?: Spirituality, Fantasy, and Superheroes* (2011), as that of "an obvious fantasy-response to the distressing mismatch between our expectations of the world and the way the world actually appears to be."[2]

As we have seen the reasons for the return of the superhero film and its indelible mark on film and popular culture are complicated and have required an engagement with the technological, industrial, economic, and ideological perspectives that have been at the heart of this project. We might speculate whether this return was one both desired and orchestrated by the film studios, distinctly aware in the first decade of the 2000s as they had once been in the 1950s that audiences all over the world were turning away from the cinema and seeking their entertainment elsewhere. We also cannot discount the fact that advances in CGI now allow filmmakers for the first time ever to put superheroes onscreen the way they were originally envisioned on the pages of the comic books which created them, not coincidentally at exactly the same time as audiences demand such spectacular action and imagery in their entertainment products more than they have ever done before.

What is clear, I hope, is that the superhero film should not be regarded as a genre of films made only for children or teenagers and certainly should not be dismissed as "not cinema," in the words of Martin Scorsese. In fact, it is clear to see that all ages, ethnicities, nationalities, genders and sexualities have found *something* that resonates for them within the genre's narratives. It is for this reason above all that the superhero renaissance is worthy of further study as it moves into its third decade with no signs of the "superhero fatigue" predicted by many. Key to this continued popularity is undoubtedly the malleability of the films in terms of themes and style, the fluidity with which they move through other genres, and how differently they are interpreted by various fans and critics. This is how *Black Panther* can be considered a "radical" and "revolutionary" film by some yet "toxic" and "racist" by others.[3] It is also how films like *Captain Marvel*, *Wonder Woman*, and *Incredibles 2* can be called feminist, sexist, and propaganda at the same time.[4]

Is it too fanciful to consider this malleability as the genre's very own superpower? That is, its ability to mutate and adapt into various forms within the United States and around the globe, all to serve the needs and demands of its audience (by way of its producers and company share-holders)? This is how it is a genre that can encompass a three-hour-long behemoth budgeted at $356 million like *Avengers: Endgame* in the same year as Todd Phillips's *Joker*, a film that was said to make sure "superhero movies will never be the same" and won the Golden Lion at the Venice Film Festival, the first in the history of the genre to have been awarded such a prestigious prize.[5] Yet it can also produce films like the modestly budgeted Italian *They Call Me Jeeg* (2015), which is as immersed in the codes and conventions of crime dramas like *Gomorrah* (2008) as it is the genre we have spent this book discussing, and the remarkable Indian film *Bhavesh Joshi: Superhero* (2018), which features social activists as super-heroes in a diegetic world as close to real as ever offered before or during the genre's renaissance. The film's two memorable protagonists, Sikander and the eponymous Bhavesh, deal with real social and political problems American superhero films refuse to even mention, let alone engage with directly. These four films are different in so many ways, but all emerge from the same shared genre foundations, which reveal the superhero film to be one much more dynamic and relevant than many have suggested.

This ability to mutate and transform could be discerned very clearly in 2018, exactly ten years after *Iron Man*, *Hancock*, and *The Dark Knight* had elevated the genre once again in the cultural imaginary and Liam Burke in his *The Comic Book Film Adaptation: Exploring Modern Hollywood's Leading Genre* (2015) suggested that it had found its "real voice."[6] 2018 will certainly be remembered as another important moment in the evo-lution of the genre, not just for its box office successes but also for the release of two major superhero films with nonwhite leads, the first since *Hancock*: T'Challa in *Black Panther* and Miles Morales in *Spider-Man: Into*

Fig. 6.1 Exploring new dimensions of the superhero genre, literally and figuratively, in *Spider-Man: Into the Spider-Verse* (2018).

Fig. 6.2 *Wonder Woman 1984* (2020): Moving into the third decade of the superhero renaissance, the genre shows no signs of the fatigue many have predicted.

the Spider-Verse. It was also in 2018 that film studios seemed to acknowledge for the first time that women had been underrepresented in the genre, with female leads in *Incredibles 2* and *Ant-Man and the Wasp* plus strong, dynamic superheroes such as Spider-Gwen in *Spider-Man: Into the Spider-Verse*; Nakia, Shuri, and Okoye in *Black Panther*; and Meera in *Aquaman*. These should not be regarded as altruistic gestures by the studios responsible, but as an awareness of the shifting coordinates of the social and political climate in which they were made, combined with a strong desire for their films to remain relevant and continue to appeal to global audiences. These are certainly indications of a tentative shift in the genre, but what the coming years will bring, of course, remains to be seen. But for now and the foreseeable future, whether we like it or not, we are living in *the age of the superhero*.

FILMOGRAPHY

Abar, the First Black Superman
(Frank Packard, 1977)
The Amazing Spider-Man (Marc
Webb, 2012)
The Amazing Spider-Man 2 (Marc
Webb, 2014)
American Hero (Nick Love, 2015)
Antboy (Ask Hasselbalch, 2013)
Antboy: Revenge of the Red Fury
(Ask Hasselbalch, 2014)
Antboy 3 (Ask Hasselbalch, 2016)
Ant-Man (Peyton Reed, 2015)
Ant-Man and the Wasp (Peyton
Reed, 2018)
Aquaman (James Wan, 2018)
The Avengers (Joss Whedon, 2012)
(in the UK: *Avengers Assemble*)
Avengers: Age of Ultron (Joss
Whedon, 2015)
Avengers: Endgame (Russo
Brothers, 2019)

Avengers: Infinity War (Russo
Brothers, 2018)
Batman (ABC, 1966–68)
Batman (Tim Burton, 1989)
Batman & Robin (Joel Schumacher,
1997)
Batman Begins (Christopher Nolan,
2005)
Batman Forever (Joel Schumacher,
1995)
Batman Returns (Tim Burton, 1992)
*Batman v Superman: Dawn of
Justice* (Zack Snyder, 2016)
Bhavesh Joshi: Superhero
(Vikramaditya Motwane, 2018)
Birdman (Alejandro G. Iñárritu,
2014)
Black Lightning (Alexandr Voytinskiy
and Dmitriy Kiselev, 2009)
Black Panther (Ryan Coogler, 2018)
Blade (Stephen Norrington, 1998)

Blade: Trinity (David S. Goyer, 2004)
Blade II (Guillermo del Toro, 2002)
Blankman (Mike Binder, 1994)
Bloodshot (David S. F. Wilson, 2020)
Brightburn (David Yarovesky, 2019)
Captain America: Civil War (Russo Brothers, 2016)
Captain America: The First Avenger (Joe Johnston, 2011)
Captain America: The Winter Soldier (Russo Brothers, 2014)
Captain Barbell (Mac Alejandre, 2003)
Captain Marvel (Anna Boden and Ryan Fleck, 2019)
Catwoman (Pitof, 2004)
Chronicle (Josh Trank, 2012)
Cicak-man (Yusry Abd Halim, 2006)
Cicak Man 2 (Yusry Abd Halim, 2008)
Cicak Man 3 (Ghaz Abu Bakar and Yusry Abd Halim, 2015)
Cobra (George P. Cosmatos, 1986)
Daredevil (Mark Steven Johnson, 2003)
The Dark Knight (Christopher Nolan, 2008)
The Dark Knight Rises (Christopher Nolan, 2012)
Dark Phoenix (Simon Kinberg, 2019)
Deadpool (Tim Miller, 2016)
Deadpool 2 (David Leitch, 2018)
Deadpool 2: The Super Duper Cut (David Leitch, 2018)

*The Death of "Superman Lives":
What Happened?* (Jon Schnepp, 2015)
Defendor (Peter Stebbings, 2009)
Doctor Strange (Scott Derrickson, 2016)
Dredd (Pete Travis, 2012)
Drona (Goldie Behl, 2008)
Elektra (Rob Bowman, 2005)
Enthiran (S. Shankar, 2010)
Fantastic Four (Tim Story, 2005)
A Flying Jatt (Remo D'Souza, 2016)
Gatchaman (Toya Sato, 2013)
Ghost Rider (Mark Steven Johnson, 2007)
Ghost Rider: Spirit of Vengeance (Mark Neveldine, 2012)
Glass (M. Night Shyamalan, 2019)
Green Lantern (Martin Campbell, 2011)
Griff the Invisible (Leon Ford, 2010)
Guardians (Sarik Andreasyan, 2017)
Guardians of the Galaxy (James Gunn, 2014)
Guardians of the Galaxy Vol. 2 (James Gunn, 2017)
Hancock (Peter Berg, 2008)
Harley Quinn: Birds of Prey (Cathy Yan, 2020)
Hellboy (Guilermo Del Toro, 2004)
Hellboy (Marshall, Neill, 2019)
Hellboy II: The Golden Army (Guilermo Del Toro, 2008)
Hulk (Ang Lee, 2003)
The Incredible Hulk (Louis Leterrier, 2008)

The Incredibles (Brad Bird, 2004)
Incredibles 2 (Brad Bird, 2018)
Iron Fist (Netflix, 2017–2018)
Iron Man (Jon Favreau, 2008)
Iron Man 2 (Jon Favreau, 2010)
Iron Man 3 (Shane Black, 2013)
Joker (Todd Phillips, 2019)
Justice League (Zack Snyder, 2017)
Kick Ass (Matthew Vaughn, 2010)
Koi . . . Mil Gaya (Rakesh Roshan, 2003)
Krrish (Rakesh Roshan, 2006)
Krrish 3 (Rakesh Roshan, 2013)
The Lego Batman Movie (Chris McKay, 2017)
Logan (James Mangold, 2017)
Man of Steel (Zack Snyder, 2013)
Max Steel (Stewart Hendler, 2016)
Megamind (Tom McGrath, 2010)
Mercury Man (Bhandit Thongdee, 2006)
The Meteor Man (Robert Townsend, 1993)
Mr India (Shekar Kapur, 1987)
My Super Ex-Girlfriend (Ivan Reitman, 2006)
The New Mutants (Josh Boone, 2020)
Once Upon a Deadpool (David Leitch, 2018)
Paper Man (Kieran and Michele Mulroney, 2009)
Pennyworth (Epix, 2019–)
The Phantom (Simon Wincer, 1996)
Prince (Kookie V. Gulati, 2010)
Psychokinesis (Yeon Sang-ho, 2018)

The Punisher (Jonathon Hensleigh, 2004)
The Punisher: War Zone (Lexi Alexander, 2008)
Ra.One (Anubhav Sinha, 2011)
Rendel (Jesse Haaja, 2017)
Secret Superstar (Advait Chandan, 2017)
Shang-Chi and the Legend of the Ten Rings (Destin Daniel Cretton, 2021)
Shazam! (David F. Sandberg, 2019)
Sky High (Mike Mitchell, 2005)
Spawn (Mark A. Z. Dippé, 1997)
Special (Hal Haberman and Jeremy Passmore, 2006)
Spider-Man (Sam Raimi, 2002)
Spider-Man: Far from Home (Jon Watts, 2019)
Spider-Man: Homecoming (Jon Watts, 2017)
Spider-Man: Into the Spider-Verse (Bob Persichetti, Peter Ramsey, and Rodney Rothman, 2018)
Spider-Man 2 (Saim Raimi, 2004)
Spider-Man 3 (Sam Raimi, 2007)
Split (M. Night Shyamalan, 2017)
Steel (Kenneth Johnson, 1997)
The Subjects (Robert Mond, 2015)
Suicide Squad (David Ayer, 2016)
The Suicide Squad (James Gunn, 2021)
Super (James Gunn, 2010)
SuperBob (Jon Drever, 2015)
Superlópez (Javier Ruiz Caldera, 2018)

Supergirl (Jeannot Szwarc, 1984)

Supergirl (CBS, 2015–)

Superheroes: A Never-Ending Battle (Michael Kantor, 2013)

Superman (B. Gupta, 1987)

Superman (Richard Donner, 1978)

Superman II (Richard Lester, 1980)

Superman III (Richard Lester, 1983)

Superman IV: The Quest for Peace (Sidney J. Furie, 1987)

Superman and the Mole Men (Lee Sholem, 1951)

Superman Returns (Bryan Singer, 2006)

Super Singh (Anurag Singh, 2017)

Tank Girl (Rachel Talalay, 1995)

Teen Titans Go! To the Movies (Aaron Horvath and Peter Rida Michail, 2018)

They Call Me Jeeg (Gabriele Mainetti, 2015)

Thor (Kenneth Branagh, 2011)

Thor: Love and Thunder (Taika Waititi, 2021)

Thor: Ragnarok (Taika Waititi, 2017)

Thor: The Dark World (Alan Foster, 2014)

2.0 (S. Shankar, 2018)

Unbreakable (M. Night Shyamalan, 2000)

Velayudham (M. Raja, 2011)

Venom (Ruben Fleischer, 2018)

Vincent Has No Scales (Thomas Salvadore, 2014)

Watchmen (Zack Snyder, 2009)

Wonder Woman (ABC/CBS, 1975–1979)

Wonder Woman (Patty Jenkins, 2017)

Wonder Woman 1984 (Patty Jenkins, 2020)

X-Men (Bryan Singer, 2000)

X-Men: Apocalypse (Bryan Singer, 2016)

X-Men: Days of Future Past (Bryan Singer, 2014)

X-Men: First Class (Matthew Vaughn, 2011)

X-Men Origins: Wolverine (Gavin Hood, 2009)

X-Men: The Last Stand (Brett Ratner, 2006)

X-Men 2 (Bryan Singer, 2003)

Zebraman (Takashi Miike, 2004)

NOTES

Introduction: Cultural Phenomenon or Cultural Catastrophe?

1. Darragh Green and Kate Roddy, introduction to *Grant Morrison and the Superhero Renaissance: Critical Essays*, ed. Darragh Green and Kate Roddy (Jefferson, NC: McFarland, 2015), 2; Steven Chermak, Frankie Y. Baily, and Michelle Brown, introduction to *Media Representations of September 11*, ed. Steven Chermak, Frankie Y. Baily, and Michelle Brown (Westport, CT: Praeger, 2003), 11; Jason Dittmer, "American Exceptionalism, Visual Effects, and the Post-9/11 Cinematic Superhero Boom," *Environment and Planning D: Society and Space* 29, no. 1 (2011): 1; Christina Adamou, "Evolving Portrayals of Masculinity in Superhero Films," in *The 21st Century Superhero: Essays on Gender, Genre, and Globalization in Film*, ed. Richard J. Gray II and Betty Kaklamanidou (Jefferson, NC: MacFarland, 2011), 94; Richard J. Gray II and Betty Kaklamanidou, introduction to *The 21st Century Superhero*, 1.

2. Liam Burke, *The Comic Book Film Adaptation: Exploring Modern Hollywood's Leading Genre* (Jackson: University of Mississippi Press, 2015), 111.

3. In 2017, four out of the top ten global earners of the year were superhero films (*Spider-Man: Homecoming, Guardians of the Galaxy Vol. 2, Thor: Ragnarok*, and *Wonder Woman*), and there were four also in 2016 (*Captain America: Civil War, Batman v Superman: Dawn of Justice, Deadpool*, and *Suicide Squad*). In 2019 the global box office top ten again featured four superhero films: *Avengers: Endgame, Spider-Man: Far From Home, Captain Marvel*, and *Joker*.

4. See James Dyer, "*Interstellar* Review," *Empire*. April 10, 2013. https://www
.empireonline.com/movies/reviews/interstellar-review/; "*Die Another Day:
Skyfall* and the Nolanization of James Bond," https://moviescene.wordpress
.com/2014/11/27/die-another-day-skyfall-and-the-nolanization-of-james-bond/.
Other films that might be included in this discussion are *Blade* (1998), *X-Men 2*
(2003), *Spider-Man 2* (2004), and *The Incredibles* (2004).

5. Quoted in Andrew Dyce, "David S. Goyer Says *Man of Steel* Will Be 'Realistic'
Like Nolan's Batman," *Screenrant.com*, January 10, 2012, http://screenrant.com
/superman-man-of-steel-realistic-david-goyer-christopher-nolan-batman/.

6. Quoted in Mike Fleming Jr., "Alejandro G. Iñárritu and 'Birdman' Scribes
on Hollywood's Superhero Fixation: 'Poison, Cultural Genocide'—Q&A,"
Deadline, October 15, 2014. http://deadline.com/2014/10/birdman-director
-alejandro-gonzalez-inarritu-writers-interview-852206/. Iñárritu's own *Birdman*
(2014) connected itself to the superhero genre in compelling ways, casting
former Batman Michael Keaton as a fading Hollywood actor remembered best
for his performance as a superhero in a trilogy of fictional Birdman films in
the 1990s.

7. Quoted in Michael Hodges, "Jodie Foster: 'My Greatest Strength Is What's in My
Head,' " *Radio Times*, January 6, 2018, https://www.radiotimes.com/news
/tv/2018-0-–06/jodie-foster-my-greatest-strength-is-whats-in-my-head/.

8. Quoted in Alison Flood, "Superheroes a 'Cultural Catastrophe', Says Comics
Guru Alan Moore." *The Guardian*, January 21, 2014, https://www.theguardian
.com/books/2014/jan/21/superheroes-cultural-catastrophe-alan-moore-comics
-watchmen.

9. Quoted in Catherine Shoard, "Ethan Hawke: superhero movies are overrated,"
The Guardian, 27 August 2018. https://www.theguardian.com/film/2018
/aug/27/ethan-hawke-superhero-movies-are-overrated-logan (accessed May 22,
2019).

10. Quoted in Jordan Zakarin, "David Cronenberg Slams Superhero Films, Calls
'Dark Knight Rises' Boring," *Hollywood Reporter*, August 15, 2012. http://www
.hollywoodreporter.com/heat-vision/david-cronenberg-slams-superhero-films
-batman-boring-362780; quoted in Zack Sharf, "Terry Gilliam Sounds Off on
Superhero Movies: 'I Hate Them. It's Bullshit. Come On, Grow Up!' " *Indiewire.
com*, June 26, 2018. https://www.indiewire.com/2018/06/terry-gilliam-superhero
-movies-hatred-bullshit-1201971699. It might be noted that Cronenberg adapted
a "comic book" with his *A History of Violence* (2005) and Gilliam once came very
close to directing an adaptation of Alan Moore's *Watchmen* (1986).

11. Susan Faludi, *The Terror Dream: Fear and Fantasy in Post-9/11 America* (Melbourne: Scribe, 2007), 51.

12. Anthony D'Alessandro, "*Avengers: Endgame* Rests at $357M+ Opening Record; Eyes $33M+ Monday & Record $180M 2nd Frame; Weekend Biz Hits $401M+ High," *Deadline*, April 29, 2019, https://deadline.com/2019/04/avengers-endgame-opening-weekend-box-office-record-1202602445/.

13. Nick de Semlyen, "*The Irishman* Week: Empire's Martin Scorsese Interview," *Empire*, November 6, 2019, https://www.empireonline.com/movies/features/irishman-week-martin-scorsese-interview/.

14. Others have been critical of Scorsese's work while simultaneously acknowledging him as one of the greatest American filmmakers of late twentieth-century American cinema. Somewhat ironically these criticisms are similar to those leveled at the superhero film: limited roles for women, formulaic narratives, and a problematic relationship with violence. See Beatrice Loayza, "Seen but Not Heard: Why Don't Women Speak in *The Irishman?*," *The Guardian*, November 7, 2019. https://www.theguardian.com/film/2019/nov/07/why-dont-women -speak-in-the-irishman-martin-scorsese-anna-paquin-hollywood; Ellis Cashmore, *Martin Scorsese's America* (Cambridge: Polity Press, 2013); Maria T. Miliora, *The Scorsese Psyche on Screen: Roots of Themes and Characters in the Films* (Jefferson, NC: McFarland, 2015).

15. Quoted in Tiffany Pritchard, " 'Scorsese Wasn't Thinking Correctly' Says Marvel Cinematographer Dante Spinotti," *Screendaily*, December 1, 2019, https://www.screendaily.com/news/scorsese-wasnt-thinking-correctly-says-marvel -cinematographer-dante-spinotti/5145209.article.

16. Quoted in Mike Fleming Jr., "George Miller on March Start Date for Next Film, More 'Mad Max', Defending Superheroes as Cinema & the Search for Depth That Makes Movies Like 'Fury Road' Unforgettable," *Deadline*, December 6, 2019, https://deadline.com/2019/12/george-miller-mad-max-fury-road-sequel-superhero-movie -debate-start-date-three-thousand-years-of-longing-interview-1202802441/.

17. Tom Gunning, "The Cinema of Attractions: Early Film, Its Spectator, and the Avant-Garde," in *Early Cinema: Space, Frame, Narrative*, ed. Thomas Elsaesser (London: British Film Institute, 1990), 58.

18. Carolyn Jess-Cooke, *Film Sequels: Theory and Practice from Hollywood to Bollywood* (Edinburgh: Edinburgh University Press, 2009), vii.

19. As an indication of the prevalence of this in modern film production, in 2018 only a single film, *Bohemian Rhapsody*, was in the top ten global box office but was not a sequel or part of a preexisting "universe"; in 2017 not a single film;

and in 2016 only two: *Zootopia* and *The Secret Life of Pets*. Also see Amanda Ann Klein and R. Barton Palmer, eds., *Cycles, Sequels, Spin-offs, Remakes, and Reboots: Multiplicities in Film and Television* (Austin: University of Texas Press, 2016).

20. Dan Jolin, "Infographic: Movie Franchise Lexicon," *Empire*, January 9, 2012, http://www.empireonline.com/movies/features/movie-franchise-lexicon -infographic/

21. In 2019 Jack Bannon starred as Alfred Pennyworth in the *Pennyworth* television series, based on the early life and adventures of the titular character before he became the long-serving butler to the Wayne family and Batman.

22. *Teen Titans Go! To the Movies* is a remarkable film for a number of reasons, just a few of which are that it features Nicolas Cage as Superman—in the same year that he played Spider-Man Noir in *Spider-Man: Into the Spider-Verse*—alongside his son (who plays a young Bruce Wayne), whom Cage named Kal-el because of his love of the character. Cage nearly played Superman in the 1990s in Tim Burton's aborted film, which is chronicled in the documentary *The Death of "Superman Lives": What Happened?* (2015). *Teen Titans Go! To the Movies* also arguably features the best of all Stan Lee's many cameos in superhero films, with an animated version of Lee, just a year before his death, yelling directly to the camera, "I don't care if it is a DC movie, I love cameos!"

23. Garyn Roberts, "Understanding the Sequential Art of Comic Strips and Comic Books and Their Descendants in the Early Years of the New Millennium," *Journal of American Culture* 27, no. 2 (2004): 210. Also see Douglas Kellner, *Cinema Wars: Hollywood Film and Politics in the Bush-Cheney Era* (Chichester: Wiley Blackwell, 2010); Francis Pheasant-Kelly, *Fantasy Film Post 9/11* (New York: Palgrave MacMillan, 2013).

24. André Bazin, "La Politique des Auteurs," in *The New Wave*, ed. Peter Graham (London: Secker and Warburg, 1968), 143–44.

25. Annika Hagley, "America's Need for Superheroes Has Led to the Rise of Donald Trump," *The Guardian*, March 28, 2016. https://www.theguardian.com /commentisfree/2016/mar/28/america-superheroes-donald-trump-brutal-comic -book-ideal; Alex Melamid, "Blame Donald Trump's Rise on the Avant-Garde Movement," *Time*, May 12, 2017, http://time.com/4777118/avant-garde -koons-trump/; Tre Johnson, "Black Panther Is a Gorgeous, Groundbreaking Celebration of Black Culture," *Vox*, February 23, 2018. https://www.vox.com /culture/2018/2/23/17028826/black-panther-wakanda-culture-marvel 2018;

Natalie Prouix, "Is *Black Panther* a 'Defining Moment' for the United States—and Particularly for Black America?," *New York Times*, March 1, 2018, https://www .nytimes.com/2018/03/01/learning/is-black-panther-a-defining-moment-for -the-united-states-and-particularly-for-black-america.html; Carvell Wallace, "Why *Black Panther* Is a Defining Moment for Black America," *New York Times Magazine*, February 12, 2018, https://www.nytimes.com/2018/02/12/magazine /why-black-panther-is-a-defining-moment-for-black-america.html2018.

26. Anne Billson, *"Man of Steel*: Are Superheroes the New Gods?," *The Telegraph*, June 17, 2013, https://www.telegraph.co.uk/culture/film/10125441/Man-of-Steel -Are-superheroes-the-new-gods.html. Also see Ben Saunders, *Do Gods Wear Capes? Spirituality, Fantasy, and Superheroes* (London: Bloomsbury, 2011).

27. De Semlyen, "*The Irishman* Week."

28. Peter Coogan, *Superhero: The Secret Origin of a Genre* (Austin, TX: Monkeybrain, 2006), 124.

29. See Dittmer, "American Exceptionalism"; Marc DiPaolo, *War, Politics, and Superheroes: Ethics and Propaganda in Comics and Film* (Jefferson, NC: McFarland, 2011).

30. Carolyn Cocca, *Superwomen: Gender, Power, and Representation* (New York: Bloomsbury, 2016), 3.

31. Anurima Chanda, "Postcolonial Responses to the Western Superhero: A Study Through Indian Nonsense Literature," *Lapis Lazuli: An International Literary Journal* 5, no. 1 (Spring 2015): 70.

32. Raminder Kauer, "The Fictions of Science and Cinema in India," in *Routledge Handbook of Indian Cinemas*, ed. K. Moti Gokulsing and Wimal Dissanayake (Abingdon, UK: Routledge, 2013), 293.

33. See Graeme McMillan, "Why *Guardians of the Galaxy* Is the Riskiest Marvel Film Since *Iron Man*," *Hollywood Reporter*, February 19, 2014, http://www .hollywoodreporter.com/heat-vision/why-guardians-galaxy-is-riskiest-681656 2014; Maana Khatchatourian, "Zack Snyder Says Batman and Superman Are Not Like 'Flavor of the Week' Ant-Man," *Variety*, September 10 2015, http://variety.com/2015/film/news/zack-snyder-batman-superman-not-flavor -of-week-ant-man-1201589800/.

34. Quoted in Graeme McMillan, "Steven Spielberg Says Superhero Movies Will Go 'the Way of the Western,' " *Hollywood Reporter*, September 2, 2015, http:// www.hollywoodreporter.com/heat-vision/steven-spielberg-predicts-superhero -movies-819768.

35. Quoted in Matt Conway, "*Avatar* Director James Cameron Hoping For 'Avengers' Fatigue," ScreenGeek.com, May 7, 2019, https://www.screengeek.net/2019/05/07 /james-cameron-avengers-fatigue/.

1. The Codes and Conventions of the Contemporary Superhero Film

1. Henry Jenkins, " 'Just Men in Tights': Rewriting Silver Age Comics in an Era of Multiplicity," in *The Shifting Definitions of Genre: Essays on Labeling Films, Television Shows, and Media*, ed. Lincoln Geraghty and Mark Jancovich (Jefferson, NC: McFarland, 2008), 231. Also see David Hyman, *Revision and the Superhero Genre* (New York: Palgrave Macmillan, 2017); Scott Bukatman, "Secret Identity Politics," in *The Contemporary Comic Book Superhero*, ed. Angela Ndalianis, 109–25 (New York: Routledge, 2009).

2. Robert Stam, *Film Theory: An Introduction* (Malden: Blackwell, 2000), 14.

3. See Annessa Ann Babic, ed., *Comics as History, Comics as Literature: Roles of the Comic Book in Scholarship, Society, and Entertainment* (Madison, NJ: Fairleigh Dickinson University Press, 2014).

4. Peter Coogan, *Superhero: The Secret Origin of a Genre* (Austin, TX: Monkeybrain, 2006), 30–33.

5. Liam Burke, *The Comic Book Film Adaptation: Exploring Modern Hollywood's Leading Genre* (Jackson: University of Mississippi Press, 2015), 111.

6. Coogan, *Superhero*, 31.

7. If one wanted the question of who beats whom answered the solution is, arguably, whoever's name is in the title of the film you are watching: thus, in *Thor: Ragnarok* Thor beats the Hulk even though he was beaten quite comprehensively by the Hulk in *The Avengers* (2012); in *Captain America: Civil War* Captain America defeats Iron Man; and in *Batman v Superman* Batman wins as it is a Batman film more than it is a Superman film.

8. In *Brightburn* Brandon Bryer is found in a crashed spaceship as a baby and adopted by human parents. His alliterative name and the symbol he chooses to represent him are common tropes of the superhero genre. Brandon has almost exactly the same powers as Superman and struggles briefly with his conscience before deciding to be *bad*. The film's tagline was "He's not here to save the world."

9. Coogan, *Superhero*, 32.

10. Coogan, *Superhero*, 31.

11. Quoted in Catherine Shoard, "*Son of Saul*'s László Nemes: 'Our Civilisation Is Preparing for Its Own Destruction,' " *The Guardian*, May 10, 2019, https://www.theguardian.com/film/2019/may/10/son-of-sauls-laszlo-nemes-our-civilisation-is-preparing-for-its-own-destruction.

12. Quoted in Kyle Kizu, "Fans Are Already Mourning the Avengers," *Hollywood Reporter*, April 19, 2019, https://www.hollywoodreporter.com/heat-vision/avengers-fans-are-mourning-endgame-deaths-1203380.

13. Quoted in 6ABC News, "Philly Audiences Find Deeper Meaning in *Black Panther*," February 16, 2018, YouTube video, https://www.youtube.com/watch?v=b4kEEpnfLrl.

14. Stephen Faller, "Iron Man's Transcendent Challenges," in *Iron Man and Philosophy*, ed. Mark D. White (Hoboken, NJ: Wiley, 2010), 259.

15. See Stefan Herbrechter, *Posthumanism: A Critical Analysis* (London: Bloomsbury, 2013); Rosa Braidotti, *The Posthuman* (Cambridge: Polity, 2013).

16. See Richard Corliss, "*2012*: End of the World Disaster Porn." *Time*, November 12, 2009, http://www.time.com/time/arts/article/0,8599,1938799,00.html.

17. See Terence McSweeney, *The 'War on Terror' and American Film: 9/11 Frames per Second* (Edinburgh: Edinburgh University Press, 2014); McSweeney, *Avengers Assemble! Critical Perspectives on the Marvel Cinematic Universe* (London: Wallflower Press, 2018).

18. Leo Braudy, *The World in a Frame: What We See in Films* (Chicago: University of Chicago Press, 2002), 111; Grant Morrison, *SuperGods: Our World in the Age of the Superhero* (London: Random House, 2011), 348.

19. Although given the character's transition from being "second string" (Geoff Boucher, "Ka-pow, Spidey!" *Los Angeles Times*, July 22, 2006, http://articles.latimes.com/2006/jul/22/entertainment/et-comic22) to perhaps the most popular superhero character in the world it is hard to imagine that Iron Man will not return to the screens in some way sooner rather than later, whether as Tony Stark or in the form of the more recent comic book iterations of the character, such as like Ironheart, a.k.a. the genius fifteen-year-old engineering student Riri Williams.

20. See Burke, *The Comic Book Film Adaptation*.

21. Lisa Purse, *Contemporary Action Cinema* (Edinburgh: Edinburgh University Press, 2011). 105.

22. See Stephen Prince, *Firestorm: American Film in the Age of Terrorism* (New York: Columbia University Press, 2009); Douglas Kellner, *Cinema Wars: Hollywood Film*

and Politics in the Bush-Cheney Era (Chichester: Wiley Blackwell, 2010); Pollard, Tom. *Hollywood 9/11: Superheroes, Supervillains, and Super Disasters* (Boulder, CO: Paradigm 2011).

23. The film also does something unprecedented in this final scene by bringing back J. K. Simmons, who had played J. Jonah Jameson in the Raimi trilogy (2002–2007), to play the same character in the MCU.

24. See Blair Davis, *Comic Book Movies* (New Brunswick, NJ: Rutgers University Press, 2018).

25. Tom Brown, *Breaking the Fourth Wall*. Edinburgh: Edinburgh University Press, 2012), 18.

26. By the way, thanks for reading this book. Is it living up to your expectations so far? Would you consider *Joker* to be a superhero film or not? There is a line about Nicolas Cage a little bit later that the publisher asked me to remove. What was the first superhero film you remember seeing? Mine was *Superman II* in London in 1980.

27. Quoted in Russ Burlingame, "*Deadpool 2* Writers Reveal Why the 'Passion of the Christ' Joke Was Risky," *Comicbook.com*, August 9, 2018, https://comicbook .com/marvel/2018/08/09/deadpool-2-writers-talk-passion-of-the-christ-joke/.

28. There are considerable differences between the three versions of the film. A few of the most notable in *Once Upon a Deadpool* are when Fred Savage challenges the film for its "fridging" of Vanessa, points out the Brad Pitt cameo for those who missed it, and suggests he wants to fight Matt Damon, which Deadpool bleeps out, making it sound as if he wants to do something else with him. *Deadpool: The Super Duper Cut* features even more gratuitous violence, extra jokes ("Let's see Captain America do that!"), alternate music tracks, and an extended ending in which Deadpool travels back in time and debates whether to kill baby Hitler or not.

2. The Mythologies of the Contemporary Superhero Film

1. Richard Slotkin, *Regeneration Through Violence* (Norman: University of Oklahoma Press, 1973), 6.

2. Arthur Asa Berger, "Comics and American Culture," in *Side-Saddle on the Golden Calf: Social Structure and Popular Culture in America*, ed. George Lewis (Pacific Palisades, CA: Goodyear, 1972), 151.

3. Will Brooker, "We Could Be Heroes," in *What Is a Superhero?*, ed. Robin S. Rosenberg and Peter Coogan (Oxford: Oxford University Press, 2013), 11.

4. John Shelton Lawrence and Robert Jewett, *The American Monomyth* (New York: Anchor/Doubleday, 1977), 48; Lawrence and Jewett, *The Myth of the American Superhero* (Grand Rapids, MI: Eerdmans, 2002).

5. Keith Spencer, "Peak Superhero? Not Even Close: How One Movie Genre Became the Guiding Myth of Neoliberalism," *Salon*, April 28, 2018, https://www .salon.com/2018/04/28/how-superhero-films-became-the-guiding-myth-of -neoliberalism/; Jason Dittmer, *Captain America and the Nationalist Superhero: Metaphors, Narratives, and Geopolitics* (Philadelphia: Temple University Press, 2012).

6. George Monbiot, "Neoliberalism—the Ideology at the Root of All Our Problems," *The Guardian*, April 15, 2016, https://www.theguardian.com/books/2016/apr/15 /neoliberalism-ideology-problem-george-monbiot.

7. Geoffrey Hodgeson, *The Myth of American Exceptionalism* (New Haven, CT: Yale University Press, 2009), 10.

8. Tanner Mirrlees, "How to Read *Iron Man*: The Economics, Politics, and Ideology of an Imperial Film Commodity," *Cineaction* 92, no. 1 (2014): 5.

9. Quoted in the documentary series *Superheroes: A Never-Ending Battle* (Michael Kantor, 2013)

10. Lawrence and Jewett, *The American Monomyth*, xx.

11. See Geoff King, *Spectacular Narratives: Hollywood in the Age of the Blockbuster* (London: I. B. Tauris, 2000).

12. Quoted in Ben Pearson, "*Logan* Is a Western Because of Audiences' Exhaustion with 'Formulaic' Superhero Movies, Says Director," *Gamesradar*, March 1, 2017, https://www.gamesradar.com/logan-is-a-western-because-of-audiences -exhaustion-with-formulaic-superhero-movies-says-director/.

13. Joshua Rivera, "*Logan* Looks Like the Superhero Western We All Need to See," *GQ*, January 19, 2017, https://www.gq.com/story/logan-looks-like-the-superhero -western-we-all-need-to-see.

14. Colin McArthur, *Underworld USA* (London: British Film Institute, 1972), 18.

15. Lisa Purse, *Contemporary Action Cinema* (Edinburgh: Edinburgh University Press, 2011), 105.

16. Jerry Siegel, quoted in Richard Reynolds, *Superheroes: A Modern Mythology* (Jackson: University Press of Mississippi, 1992), 9; Chris Rojek, *Celebrity* (London: Reaktion, 2001), 25.

17. See Ian Gordon, *Superman: The Persistence of an American Icon* (New Brunswick, NJ: Rutgers University Press, 2017).

18. Francis Pheasant-Kelly, *Fantasy Film Post 9/11* (New York: Palgrave MacMillan, 2013), 144.

19. See Travis Langley, ed., *Batman and Psychology: A Dark and Stormy Knight* (Hoboken, NJ: Wiley, 2012); Will Brooker, *Hunting The Dark Knight: Twenty-First Century Batman* (London: I. B. Tauris, 2012); Roberta Pearson, William Uricchio, and Will Brooker, eds. *Many More Lives of the Batman* (London: British Film Institute, 2015); Alex M. Wainer *Soul of the Dark Knight: Batman as Mythic Figure in Comics and Film* (Jefferson, NC: MacFarland,, 2014); Dan Hassler-Forrest. *Capitalist Superheroes: Caped Crusaders in the Neoliberal Age* (London: Zero, 2013); Liam Burke, ed. *Fan Phenomena Batman* (Bristol: I. B Tauris, 2013); Bart Beatty, "Don't Ask, Don't Tell: How Do You Illustrate an Academic Essay About Batman and Homosexuality?" *Comics Journal* no. 228 (2000): 17–18; Andy Medhurst, "Batman, Deviance, and Camp," in *The Many Lives of the Batman: Critical Approaches to a Superhero and His Media*, ed. Roberta E. Pearson and William Uricchio (London: Routledge, 1991), 149–63.

20. Denis O'Neill, introduction to *Batman and Psychology: A Dark and Stormy*, ed. Travis Langley (Hoboken, NJ: Wiley, 2012), 1.

21. Wainer, *Soul of the Dark Knight*, 127.

22. Ron Pennington, review of *Batman*, *Hollywood Reporter*, June 23, 1989, https://www.hollywoodreporter.com/news/batman-thrs-1989-review-801339.

23. Quoted in Tim Lowery, "Five Lessons Hollywood Learned from Tim Burton's *Batman* (1989)," RottenTomatoes.com, June 23 2019, https://editorial.rottentomatoes .com/article/five-lessons-hollywood-learned-from-tim-burtons-batman -1989/.

24. See Justine Toh, "The Tools and Toys of (the) War (on Terror): Consumer Desire, Military Fetish, and Regime Change in *Batman Begins*," in *Reframing 9/11: Film, Popular Culture, and the 'War on Terror,'* ed. Jeff Birkenstein, Anna Froula, and Karen Randell (London: Continuum, 2010), 127–39; and Christine Muller, "Power, Choice, and September 11 in *The Dark Knight*," in *The 21st Century Superhero: Essays on Gender, Genre, and Globalization in Film*, ed. Richard J. Gray and Betty Kaklamanidou (Jefferson, NC: MacFarland, 2011), 46–59.

25. Quoted in Tom Ryan, "In Defence of Big, Expensive Films," The Age, July 14, 2005, http://www.theage.com.au/news/film/defending-the blockbuster/2005/07/14 /1120934352863.html.

26. Andrew O'Hehir, "*The Dark Knight Rises*: Christopher Nolan's Evil Masterpiece," *Salon.com*, July 18, 2012, http://www.salon.com/2012/07/18/the_dark_knight _rises_christopher_nolans_evil_masterpiece/.

27. Dick Cheney, quoted in *Meet the Press*, NBC, September 16, 2001.

28. Michael Caine, quoted in Benjamin Svetkey, "Q+A Director's Chair," *Entertainment Weekly*, July 25, 2008, http://www.ew.com/ew/article/0,,20215252,00.html.

29. Rob Salkowitz, "*Batman v Superman* Is A Blockbuster for the Trump Era," *Forbes*, March 28, 2016, https://www.forbes.com/sites/robsalkowitz/2016/03/28/batman-v-superman-is-a-blockbuster-for-the-trump-era/#530f3cb94cb6.

30. Quoted in John Harwood, "Pay Attention to the Man Behind the Curtain: Trump Is No Wizard of Government," CNBC.com, April 28, 2017, https://www.cnbc.com/2017/04/28/pay-attention-to-the-man-behind-the-curtain-trump-is-no-wizard-of-government.html. Also see Chris Mandle, "Donald Trump Tells Naive Child 'I Am Batman' Despite Not Actually Being Batman," *Independent*, August 17, 2015, https://www.independent.co.uk/news/people/donald-trump-tells-naive-child-i-am-batman-despite-not-actually-being-batman-10459503.html

3. Gender and Sexuality in the Contemporary Superhero Film

1. In the decades before this other superhero films with female leads, such as *Supergirl* (1984), *Tank Girl* (1995), and *Barb Wire* (1996), had all struggled at the box office and with critics.

2. Stacy L. Smith et al., "Inequality in 800 Popular Films: Examining Portrayals of Gender, Race, & LGBT Status from 2007 to 2015," Media, Diversity, and Social Change Initiative, USC Annenberg, 2016, https://annenberg.usc.edu/sites/default/files/2017/04/10/MDSCI_Inequality_in_800_Films_FINAL.pdf; Smith et al., "Inequality in 700 Popular Films: Examining Portrayals of Gender, Race, & LGBT Status from 2007 to 2014," Media, Diversity, and Social Change Initiative, USC Annenberg, 2015, http://assets.uscannenberg.org/docs/inequality_in_700_popular_films_8215_final_for_posting.pdf.

3. Stacy L. Smith et al., "Inclusion in the Director's Chair? Gender, Race, & Age of Film Directors Across 1,000 Films from 2007–2016," Media, Diversity, and Social Change Initiative, USC Annenberg, 2017, http://annenberg.usc.edu/pages/~/media/MDSCI/Inclusion%20in%20the%20Directors%20Chair%202117%20Final.ashxhttp://annenberg.usc.edu/pages/~/media/MDSCI/Inclusion%20in%20the%20Directors%20Chair%202117%20Final.ashx.

4. Martha M. Lauzen, "It's a Man's (Celluloid) World: Portrayals of Female Characters in the Top 100 Films of 2017," Center for the Study of Women in Television and Film, San Diego State University, 2018, https://womenintvfilm.sdsu.edu/wp-content/uploads/2018/03/2017_Its_a_Mans_Celluloid_World_Report_3.pdf.

5. See Andres DeLeon, "*Captain Marvel*: Manage Your Expectations." *Libertarian Republic*, March 24, 2019, https://thelibertarianrepublic.com/captain-marvel -manage-your-expectations; Austin Frank, "It Is Your Patriotic Duty to Make Sure Disney's Feminist Propaganda Piece Captain Marvel Bombs," *Today in Politics*, March 5, 2019, https://tipolitics.com/2019/03/05/it-is-your-patriotic-duty-to -make-sure-disneys-feminist-propaganda-piece-captain-marvel-bombs/; Wlad Sarmiento, "The Standard Badass Superhero of Captain Marvel," *Chicago Maroon*, March 21, 2019, https://www.chicagomaroon.com/article/2019/3/21 /standard-badass-superhero-captain-marvel/ 2019); Polite Leader, "*Captain Marvel* Movie Analysis," March 23, 2019, https://www.youtube.com/watch?v =xIaOP3kpI58. The film's much more interesting narrative subtext connects it to the Trump era's demonization of immigrants and the fabricated border crisis that emerged as one of the cornerstones of his campaign and presidency. The Kree are sold a war against refugees by comments from the Supreme Intelligence like, "Thanks to you [Carol] those insidious shapeshifters will threaten our borders no more."

6 GLAAD Media Institute, "2018 GLAAD Studio Responsibility Index," 2018, https:// www.glaad.org/files/2018%20GLAAD%20Studio%20Responsibility%20Index .pdf., 3, 9.

7. Quoted in Sophie Zeldin-O'Neill and Jonross Swaby, ' "There Are Gay Characters in the Marvel Universe': Guardians of the Galaxy Vol 2 Cast and Crew Interviewed— Video," *The Guardian*, May 1, 2017, https://www.theguardian.com/film/video /2017/may/01/gay-characters-marvel-guardians-of-the-galaxy-vol-2-chris-pratt -karen-gillan.

8. Joe Russo, quoted in Emma Kelly, "*Avengers: Endgame* Directors Russo Brothers Dragged for Their Attempt at LGBTQ+ Representation," *Metro*, April 29, 2019, https://metro.co.uk/2019/04/29/avengers-endgame-directors-russo-brothers -dragged-attempt-lgbtq-representation-9335307/; Justin Kirkland, "The Gay Avengers: Endgame Character Is a Half-Baked Attempt at Diversity," *Esquire*, May 1, 2019, https://www.esquire.com/entertainment/movies/a27334096 /avengers-endgame-gay-representation/.

9. Lisa Purse, *Contemporary Action Cinema* (Edinburgh: Edinburgh University Press, 2011), 144–45. Also see Cavan Sieczkowski, "Ian McKellen Took *X-Men* Role Because of Gay Rights Parallel," *Huffington Post*, February 27, 2014. https://www .huffingtonpost.co.uk/2014/02/27/ian-mckellen-x-men-gay_n_4865739.html 2014; Marc DiPaolo, *War, Politics, and Superheroes: Ethics and Propaganda in Comics and Film* (Jefferson, NC: McFarland, 2011).

10. Fabian Nicieza (@FabianNicieza), Twitter, August 12, 2015, 4:09 p.m., https:// twitter.com/FabianNicieza/status/631482629494149121.

11. Francesca Coppa, *The Fanfiction Reader: Folktales for the Digital Age* (Ann Arbor: University of Michigan Press, 2017), 205–6. In one such short story, "Brooklyn" (2014), an author using the name togina, writes, "Bucky shrugged, tilted his head, and smiled at the world. 'Okay. Captain America, what's your stance on gay marriage?' 'Oh God, you jerk,' Steve retorted, laughing helplessly, leaning in to kiss his best friend—his fiancé—on a street in New York, on cameras broadcasting around the world." Togina, "Brooklyn," Archiveofourown.com May 21, 2014, https://archiveofourown.org/works/1669439.

12. Kevin Feige, quoted in Caroline Westbrooke, "There's Going to Be an LGBT Superhero in the Marvel Cinematic Universe," *Metro*, June 30, 2015, https:// metro.co.uk/2015/06/30/just-when-the-marvel-cinematic-universe-introduce -an-lgbtq-character-kevin-feige-says-itll-be-within-a-decade-5272298/. Also see Gregory Ellwood, "Kevin Feige Says There Will Soon Be at Least Two LGBTQ Heroes in Marvel Universe," *ThePlaylist.net*, June 25, 2018, https://theplaylist.net/kevin -feige-lgbtq-marvel-universe-20180625/.

13. Zoe Williams, "Why *Wonder Woman* Is a Masterpiece of Subversive Feminism," *The Guardian*, June 5, 2017, https://www.theguardian.com/lifeandstyle/2017 /jun/05/why-wonder-woman-is-a-masterpiece-of-subversive-feminism; Henry D. Godinez, "Why Wonder Woman Is the Perfect Hero for the Trump Era," *Washington Post*, June 29, 2017, https://www.washingtonpost.com/news /posteverything/wp/2017/06/29/why-wonder-woman-is-the-perfect-hero-for -the-trump-era/; George Kolias, "Wonder Woman in the Age of Trump," *Huffington Post*, June 9, 2017, https://www.huffingtonpost.com/entry/wonder -woman-in-the-age-of-trump_us_593a46dae4b094fa859f1766.

14. Frederic Wertham, *Seduction of the Innocent* (New York: Rinehart, 1954), 34; Ruth McClelland-Nugent, " 'Steve Trevor, Equal?' Wonder Woman in an Era of Second Wave Feminist Critique," in *The Ages of Wonder Woman: Essays on the Amazon Princess in Changing Times*, ed. Joseph Darowski (Jefferson, NC: McFarland, 2014), 136; and Gloria Steinem, "Wonder Woman" (1972), in *The Superhero Reader*, ed. Charles Hatfield, Jeet Heer, and Kent Worcester (Jackson: University of Mississippi Press, 2013), 208.

15. Leonard Maltin, "I Wonder What's Wrong with 'Wonder Woman,'" *LeonardMaltin.com*, June 1, 2017, http://leonardmaltin.com/i-wonder-whats-wrong-with-wonder-woman/.

16. Williams, "Why *Wonder Woman* Is a Masterpiece of Subversive Feminism"; Paula Simons, "Get Us Out from Under, Wonder Woman," *Edmonton Journal*,

June 2, 2017, https://edmontonjournal.com/opinion/columnists/paula-simons
-get-us-out-from-under-wonder-woman; Josephine Livingstone, "Wonder Woman
Is Propaganda," *New Republic*, June 6, 2017, https://newrepublic.com/article
/143100/wonder-woman-propaganda.

17. David Price, *The Pixar Touch: The Making of a Company* (New York: Vintage,
2009).

18. In 2005 Disney released *Sky High*, which has a similar plot but follows the
story of the Commander and his son, Will Stronghold, rather than his mother,
Jetstream.

19. Charlie Ridgely, "Brad Bird Reveals Why Each 'Incredibles' Character Has Their
Specific Power," *Comicbook.com*, April 16, 2018, https://comicbook.com
/movies/2018/04/15/why-incredibles-have-specific-powers-pixar-brad-bird/.

20. Eric Herhuth, *Pixar and the Aesthetic Imagination: Animation, Storytelling, and
Digital Culture* (Berkeley: University of California Press, 2017), 139–40.

21. Deitmar Meinel, *Pixar's America: The Re-Animation of American Myths and
Symbols* (New York: Palgrave Macmillan, 2018), 171.

22. Quoted in Anna Smith, "How *Incredibles 2* Goes to Work for the Feminist
Superhero," *The Guardian*, June 28, 2018, https://www.theguardian.com
/film/2018/jun/28/incredibles-2-feminism-animation.

4. Ethnicity in the Contemporary Superhero Film

1. Going back slightly further we have *The Meteor Man* (1993), *Blankman* (1994),
Spawn (1997), and *Steel* (1997). If we take into account smaller roles in
larger films we can include the likes of the several black characters in the X
Men franchise (2000–), although none of whom could be called a lead, *The
Incredibles* (2004), *Suicide Squad* (2016), and *Justice League* (2017). We can also
mention the Blaxploitation film *Abar, the First Black Superman* (1977), which is
considered the first superhero film with an African American lead.

2. Stacy L. Smith et al., "Inequality in 1,100 Popular Films: Examining Portrayals
of Gender, Race/Ethnicity, LGBT, and Disability from 2007 to 2017," Annenberg
Foundation and USC Annenberg Inclusion Institute, July 2018, http://assets
.uscannenberg.org/docs/inequality-in-1100-popular-films.pdf, 15.

3. Jamie Smith, "The Revolutionary Power of *Black Panther*," *Time*, February 11,
2019, http://time.com/black-panther/.

4. Adilifu Nama, *Super Black: American Pop Culture and Black Superheroes* (Austin:
University of Texas Press, 2011), 137.

5. Ada Tseng, "The Complex History of Asian Americans in Movies, from the Silent Era to *Crazy Rich Asians*," *Washington Post*, August 8, 2018. https://www .washingtonpost.com/entertainment/the-complex-history-of-asian-americans -in-movies-from-the-silent-era-to-crazy-rich-asians/2018/08/08/77bc4176-9666 -11e8-810c-5fa705927d54_story.html.

6. Ahnar Karim, "The Marvel Cinematic Universe Is 61% White, but Does That Matter?," *Forbes*, October 10, 2018, https://www.forbes.com/sites /anharkarim/2018/10/10/ the-marvel-cinematic-universe-is-61-white-but-does-that-matter/#fb5d9cc4482e.

7. See Matthew C. Whitaker, *Icons of Black America: Breaking Barriers and Crossing Boundaries* (Santa Barbara, CA: ABC-CLIO, 2011).

8. Jeffrey Brown, *The Modern Superhero in Film and Television: Popular Genre and American Culture* (New York: Routledge, 2016), 127.

9. Erica Chito Childs, *Fade to Black and White: Interracial Images in Popular Culture* (Lanham, MD: Rowman and Littlefield, 2009), 186.

10. Marc DiPaolo, *War, Politics, and Superheroes: Ethics and Propaganda in Comics and Film*. Jefferson, NC: McFarland, 2011), 244.

11. Daniel O'Brien, *Black Masculinity on Film: Native Sons and White Lies* (New York: Palgrave Macmillan, 2017), 193.

12. Brown, *The Modern Superhero in Film and Television*, 128–29.

13. Carvell Wallace, "Why *Black Panther* Is a Defining Moment for Black America," *New York Times Magazine*, February 12, 2018, https://www.nytimes.com /2018/02/12/magazine/why-black-panther-is-a-defining-moment-for-black -america.html; Natalie Prouix, "Is *Black Panther* a 'Defining Moment' for the United States—and Particularly for Black America?" *New York Times*, March 1, 2018, https://www.nytimes.com/2018/03/01/learning/is-black-panther-a -defining-moment-for-the-united-states-and-particularly-for-black-america .html; Leonard Pitts Jr., "*Black Panther* a Watershed in Cultural History of African Americans," *Miami Herald*, February 15, 2018, https://www.miamiherald.com /opinion/opn-columns-blogs/leonard-pitts-jr/article200350754.html; Brentlin Mock, "*Black Panther* Marks Milestone in Black Culture's Impact on Hollywood," NBCNews.com, February 11, 2018. https://www.nbcnews.com/pop-culture /movies/black-panther-marks-milestone-black-culture-s-impact-hollywood -n846891; Issac Bailey, "Black Panther Is for Film What Barrack Obama Was for the Presidency," CNN.com, February 9, 2018, https://edition.cnn.com /2018/02/09/opinions/black-panther-black-america-donald-trump-bailey -opinion/index.html.

14. Quoted in Nick de Semlyen, "*The Irishman* Week: Empire's Martin Scorsese Interview," *Empire*, November 6, 2019, https://www.empireonline.com/movies/features/irishman-week-martin-scorsese-interview/.

15. Ytasha Womack, *Afrofuturism: The World of Black Sci-Fi and Fantasy Culture* (Chicago: Lawrence Hill, 2013), 9. Also see Mark Derry, "Black to the Future: Interviews with Samuel A. Delaney, Greg Tate, and Tricia Rose," in *Flame Wars: The Discourse of Cyberculture*, ed. Mark Derry (Durham, NC: Duke University Press, 1994), 179–222.

16. Ignatiy Vishnevetsky, "The Entertaining and Ambitious *Black Panther* Breaks from the Marvel Formula," *A.V. Club*, February 14, 2018, https://www.avclub.com/the-entertaining-and-ambitious-black-panther-breaks-fro-1822976016; Slavoj Žižek, "Quasi Duo Fantasias: A Straussian Reading of *Black Panther*," *Los Angeles Review of Books*, March 3, 2018, https://lareviewofbooks.org/article/quasi-duo-fantasias-straussian-reading-black-panther/. Also see Carrie Wittmer, "The Top 22 Marvel Cinematic Universe Villains, Ranked from Worst to Best," *Business Insider*, July 23, 2018, https://www.businessinsider.com/marvel-cinematic-universe-villains-ranked-from-worst-to-best-2018-2; Conner Schwerdtfeger, "Is Michael B. Jordan's Killmonger Marvel's Best Villain Yet?," Cinemablend.com, February 16, 2018, https://www.cinemablend.com/news/2312522/is-michael-b-jordans-killmonger-marvels-best-villain-yet.

17. Manohla Dargis, "Review: 'Black Panther' Shakes Up the Marvel Universe," *New York Times*, February 6, 2018. https://www.nytimes.com/2018/02/06/movies/black-panther-review-movie.html; Tim Grierson, review of *Black Panther*, *Screen Daily*, February 6, 2018, https://www.screendaily.com/reviews/black-panther-review/5126078.article.

5. The Global Contemporary Superhero Film

1. Elizabeth Ezra and Terry Rowden, *Transnational Cinema: The Film Reader* (Abingdon, Oxon: Routledge, 2006), 2.

2. Phil de Semlyen, "Exclusive: *SuperBob* Trailer Soars Online," *Empire*, September 24, 2015, https://www.empireonline.com/movies/news/exclusive-superbob-trailer-soars-online/. Also see Pamela McClintock, "$200 Million and Rising: Hollywood Struggles with Soaring Marketing Costs." *Hollywood Reporter*, July 31, 2014, https://www.hollywoodreporter.com/news/200-million-rising-hollywood-struggles-721818.

3. See Jessica Rawden, "How Much Pirates of the Caribbean Movies Have Shelled Out Just for Snacks," Cinemablend.com, May 28, 2017, https://www.cinemablend .com/news/1664249/how-much-pirates-of-the-caribbean-movies-have-shelled -out-just-for-snacks; Jacob Oller, "Shazam's Suit Cost Over $1 Million Dollars— and They Made 10 of Them," Syfy.com, January 15, 2019, https://www.syfy.com /syfywire/shazams-suit-cost-over-1-million-dollars-and-they-made-10-of-them.

4. See Martha P. Nochimson, *World on Film: An Introduction* (Oxford: Wiley-Blackwell, 2011).

5. "8 Malaysian-Made Films That Every Malaysian Should Know," KLIPS+, 2016, http://blog.klips.my/post/121083180387/8malaysianmadefilmklips.

6. See Hannah Ellis-Petersen, "Malaysia Accused of 'State-Sponsored Homophobia' After LGBT Crackdown." *The Guardian*, August 22, 2018, https://www.theguardian .com/world/2018/aug/22/ malaysia-accused-of-state-sponsored-homophobia-after-lgbt-crackdown.

7. See Emir Zainul, "Website Blocking in Malaysia Has Reduced Online Piracy, Says Film Makers Body," *Edge Markets*, October 10, 2017, http://www.theedgemarkets.com/article/ website-blocking-malaysia-has-reduced-online-piracy-says-film-makers-body.

8. Iain Robert Smith, *The Hollywood Meme: Transnational Adaptations in World Cinema* (Edinburgh: Edinburgh University Press, 2018), 12.

9. Nick Cullather, *Illusions of Influence* (Stanford, CA: Stanford University Press, 1994), 2. Also see Faye Caronan, *Legitimizing Empire: Filipino American and U.S. Puerto Rican Cultural Critique* (Chicago: University of Illinois Press, 2015).

10. See Emil M. Flores, "The Concept of the Superhero in Filipino Films," *Plaridel* 2, no. 2 (August 2005): 23–38.

11. Richard Gray, review of *Psychokinesis*, *Reel Bits*, April 28, 2018, https://thereelbits .com/2018/04/25/review-psychokinesis/.

12. See Dan Hassler-Forrest, *Capitalist Superheroes: Caped Crusaders in the Neoliberal Age* (London: Zero, 2012).

13. Peter Coogan, *Superhero: The Secret Origin of a Genre* (Austin, TX: Monkeybrain, 2006), 31.

14. Quoted in "Insider's P.O.V: Jon Drever, Director of *SuperBob*," *Callsheet*, n.d., http://www.thecallsheet.co.uk/news/insiders-pov-jon-drever-director-superbob, accessed September 21, 2019.

15. The main difference between the short and the feature is that in the short film there are references to other well-known superheroes which may have been

impossible to use in the feature because of copyright restrictions. Bob informs us that he had met Batman recently, "He was round for dinner the other night, had a lovely chat . . . still *very* angry about the death of his parents."

16. See Richard Wallace, *Mockumentary Comedy: Performing Authenticity* (New York: Palgrave Macmillan, 2019).

17. I. Q. Hunter and Laraine Porter, introduction to *British Comedy Cinema*, ed. I. Q. Hunter and Laraine Porter (New York: Routledge, 2012), 2.

18. Cynthia J.Miller, ed. *Too Bold for the Box Office: The Mockumentary from Big Screen to Small* (Lanham, MD: Scarecrow, 2012), xi.

19. Anuparma Chopra, "*Krrish 3* Ultimately Belongs to Hrithik," *Hindustan Times*, November 5, 2013, https://www.hindustantimes.com/movie-reviews/movie -review-by-anupama-chopra-krrish-3-ultimately-belongs-to-hrithik/story -Yjdoq74UbMhUjhWXxY7qXJ.html.

20. Shekhar Kapur, quoted in Anuparma Chopra, "In *Krrish*, Bollywood Gets a Superhero of Its Own," *New York Times*, June 11, 2006, https://www.nytimes .com/2006/06/11/movies/in-krrish-bollywood-gets-a-superhero-of-its-own.html.

21. Sujay Kumar, "*Krrish 3* Review: What the Bollywood Movie Steals from Superhero Films," *Daily Beast*, August 11, 2013, https://www.thedailybeast.com /krrish-3-review-what-the-bollywood-movie-steals-from-superhero-films.

22. Carolyne Jess-Cooke, *Film Sequels: Theory and Practice from Hollywood to Bollywood* (Edinburgh: Edinburgh University Press, 2009), 119. Also see Thomas Shibu, "TV Writer Seeks Stay on *Ra.One*," *Times of India*, October 21, 2011.,https://timesofindia.indiatimes.com/city/mumbai/TV-writer-seeks-stay -on-Ra-One/articleshow/10434305.cms.

Conclusion: "Is it me or is it getting crazier out there?": The Future of the Contemporary Superhero Film and the Genre's "Impossible Solutions for Insoluble Problems

1. John Shelton Lawrence, and Robert Jewett, *The Myth of the American Superhero* (Grand Rapids, MI: Eerdmans, 2002), xx. For the four countries mentioned: Australia has the likes of *Griff the Invisible* (2010) and *The Subjects* (2015); Japan has *Zebraman* (2004) and *Gatchaman* (2013); Russia has *Guardians* (2017) and *Black Lightning* (2009); and Zambia has the TV show *Mama K's Team 4* (Netflix, 2019–).

2. Ben Saunders, *Do Gods Wear Capes? Spirituality, Fantasy, and Superheroes* (London: Bloomsbury, 2011), 5.

3. Mark Powell, "The Radical Politics of *Black Panther*," *Spectator*, February 26,
    2018, https://www.spectator.com.au/2018/02/the-radical-politics-of-black
    -panther/; Jamil Smith, "The Revolutionary Power of *Black Panther*," *Time*,
    February 11, 2019, http://time.com/black-panther/; Nonso Obikili, "Toxic
    Economics and Politics: The *Black Panther* Edition," *Nonso Obikili's Blog*,
    February 23, 2018, https://nonsoobikili.wordpress.com/2018/02/23/toxic
    -economics-and-politics-the-black-panther-edition/; Christopher LeBron,
    "*Black Panther* Is Not the Movie We Deserve," Boston Review, February 17, 2018,
    http://bostonreview.net/race/christopher-lebron-black-panther.
4. See Cee Cee Elle, "Wonder Woman Is Not a Feminist Movie," *Medium*, June 19,
    2017, https://medium.com/@ceeceeelle/wonder-woman-is-not-a-feminist-movie
    -6d1071fb980f; Andres DeLeon, "*Captain Marvel*: Manage Your Expectations,"
    Libertarian Republic, March 24, 2019, https://thelibertarianrepublic.com/captain
    -marvel-manage-your-expectations; Austin Frank, "It Is Your Patriotic Duty to
    Make Sure Disney's Feminist Propaganda Piece Captain Marvel Bombs," *Today in
    Politics*, March 5, 2019, https://tipolitics.com/2019/03/05/it-is-your-patriotic
    -duty-to-make-sure-disneys-feminist-propaganda-piece-captain-marvel-bombs/.
5. David Ehrlich, " 'Joker' Review: For Better or Worse, Superhero Movies Will Never
    Be the Same," *Indiewire*, August 31, 2019, https://www.indiewire.com/2019/08
    /joker-review-joaquin-phoenix-1202170236/.
6. Liam Burke, *The Comic Book Film Adaptation: Exploring Modern Hollywood's
    Leading Genre* (Jackson: University of Mississippi Press, 2015), 111.

BIBLIOGRAPHY

Adamou, Christina. "Evolving Portrayals of Masculinity in Superhero Films." In *The 21st Century Superhero Essays on Gender, Genre and Globalization in Film*, edited by Richard J. Gray II and Betty Kaklamanidou, 94–109. Jefferson, NC: MacFarland, 2011.

Andelman, Bob. *Will Eisner: A Spirited Life*. Raleigh, NC: TwoMorrows, 2005.

Babic, Annessa Ann, ed. *Comics as History, Comics as Literature: Roles of the Comic Book in Scholarship, Society, and Entertainment*. Madison, NJ: Fairleigh Dickinson University Press, 2014.

Bailey, Issac. "Black Panther Is for Film What Barrack Obama Was for the Presidency." CNN.com, February 9, 2018. https://edition.cnn.com/2018/02/09/opinions/black-panther-black-america-donald-trump-bailey-opinion/index.html.

Bazin, André. "La Politique des Auteurs." In *The New Wave*, edited by Peter Graham, 143–44. London: Secker and Warburg, 1968.

Beatty, Bart. "Don't Ask, Don't Tell: How Do You Illustrate an Academic Essay About Batman and Homosexuality?" *Comics Journal* no. 228 (2000): 17–18.

Berger, Arthur Asa. "Comics and American Culture." In *Side-Saddle on the Golden Calf: Social Structure and Popular Culture in America*, edited by George Lewis. Pacific Palisades, CA: Goodyear, 1972.

Billson, Anne. "Man of Steel: Are Superheroes the New Gods?" *The Telegraph*, June 17, 2013. https://www.telegraph.co.uk/culture/film/10125441/Man-of-Steel-Are-superheroes-the-new-gods.html.

Boucher, Geoff. "Ka-pow, Spidey!" *Los Angeles Times*, July 22, 2006. http://articles.latimes.com/2006/jul/22/entertainment/et-comic22.

Braidotti, Rosa. *The Posthuman*. Cambridge: Polity, 2013.

Braudy, Leo. *The World in a Frame: What We See in Films*. Chicago: University of Chicago Press, 2002.

Brooker, Will. "We Could Be Heroes." In *What Is a Superhero?*, edited by Robin S. Rosenberg and Peter Coogan, 11–17. Oxford: Oxford University Press, 2013.

——. *Hunting The Dark Knight: Twenty-First Century Batman*. London: I. B. Tauris, 2012.

Brown, Jeffrey. *The Modern Superhero in Film and Television: Popular Genre and American Culture*. New York: Routledge, 2016.

Brown, Tom. *Breaking the Fourth Wall*. Edinburgh: Edinburgh University Press, 2012.

Bukatman, Scott. "Secret Identity Politics." In *The Contemporary Comic Book Superhero*, edited by Angela Ndalianis, 109–25. New York: Routledge, 2009.

Burke, Liam. *The Comic Book Film Adaptation: Exploring Modern Hollywood's Leading Genre*. Jackson: University of Mississippi Press, 2015.

Burke, Liam, ed. *Fan Phenomena Batman*. Bristol: I. B. Tauris, 2013.

Burlingame, Russ. "*Deadpool 2* Writers Reveal Why the 'Passion of the Christ' Joke Was Risky." *Comicbook.com*, August 9, 2018. https://comicbook.com/marvel/2018/08/09/deadpool-2-writers-talk-passion-of-the-christ-joke/.

Caronan, Faye. *Legitimizing Empire: Filipino American and U.S. Puerto Rican Cultural Critique*. Chicago: University of Illinois Press, 2015.

Cashmore, Ellis. *Martin Scorsese's America*. Cambridge: Polity Press, 2013.

Chanda, Anurima. "Postcolonial Responses to the Western Superhero: A Study Through Indian Nonsense Literature." *Lapis Lazuli: An International Literary Journal* 5, no. 1 (Spring 2015): 68–89.

Chermak, Steven, Frankie Y. Baily, and Michelle Brown. Introduction to *Media Representations of September 11*, edited by Steven Chermak, Frankie Y. Baily, and Michelle Brown, 1–14. Westport, CT: Praeger, 2003.

Child, Ben. "Captain Marvel: why sexist attempts at sabotage will fail." *The Guardian*, February 21, 2019. https://www.theguardian.com/film/2019/feb/21/captain-marvel-why-sexist-attempts-at-sabotage-will-fail.

Childs, Erica Chito. *Fade to Black and White: Interracial Images in Popular Culture*. Lanham, MD: Rowman and Littlefield, 2009.

Chopra, Anuparma. "In *Krrish*, Bollywood Gets a Superhero of Its Own." *New York Times*, June 11, 2006. https://www.nytimes.com/2006/06/11/movies/in-krrish-bollywood-gets-a-superhero-of-its-own.html.

——. "*Krrish 3* Ultimately Belongs to Hrithik." *Hindustan Times*, November 5, 2013. https://www.hindustantimes.com/movie-reviews/movie-review-by-anupama-chopra-krrish-3-ultimately-belongs-to-hrithik/story-Yjdoq74UbMhUjhWXxY7qXJ.html.

Cocca, Carolyn. *Superwomen: Gender, Power, and Representation*. New York: Bloomsbury, 2016.

Conway, Matt. "*Avatar* Director James Cameron Hoping For 'Avengers' Fatigue.'" ScreenGeek.com, May 7, 2019. https://www.screengeek.net/2019/05/07 /james-cameron-avengers-fatigue/.

Coogan, Peter. *Superhero: The Secret Origin of a Genre*. Austin, TX: Monkeybrain, 2006.

Coppa, Francesca. *The Fanfiction Reader: Folktales for the Digital Age*. Ann Arbor: University of Michigan Press, 2017.

Corliss, Richard. "*2012*: End of the World Disaster Porn." *Time*, November 12, 2009. http://www.time.com/time/arts/article/0,8599,1938799,00.html.

Cullather, Nick. *Illusions of Influence*. Stanford, CA: Stanford University Press, 1994.

D'Alessandro, Anthony. "*Avengers: Endgame* Rests at $357M+ Opening Record; Eyes $33M + Monday & Record $180M 2nd Frame; Weekend Biz Hits $401M+ High." *Deadline*, April 29, 2019. https://deadline.com/2019/04/avengers-endgame-opening-weekend -box-office-record-1202602445/.

Dargis, Manohla. "Review: 'Black Panther' Shakes Up the Marvel Universe." *New York Times*, February 6, 2018. https://www.nytimes.com/2018/02/06/movies/black -panther-review-movie.html.

Davis, Blair. *Comic Book Movies*. New Brunswick, NJ: Rutgers University Press, 2018.

DeLeon, Andres. "*Captain Marvel*: Manage Your Expectations." *Libertarian Republic*, March 24, 2019. https://thelibertarianrepublic.com/captain-marvel-manage -your-expectations.

Denison, Rayna, and Rachel Mizsei-Ward, eds. *Superheroes on World Screens*. Jackson: University Press of Mississippi, 2011.

Derry, Mark. "Black to the Future: Interviews with Samuel A. Delaney, Greg Tate, and Tricia Rose." In *Flame Wars: The Discourse of Cyberculture*, 179–222. Edited by Mark Derry. Durham, NC: Duke University Press, 1994.

de Semlyen, Nick. "*The Irishman* Week: Empire's Martin Scorsese Interview." *Empire*, November 6, 2019. https://www.empireonline.com/movies/features /irishman-week-martin-scorsese-interview/.

de Semlyen, Phil. "Exclusive: *SuperBob* Trailer Soars Online." *Empire*, September 24, 2015. https://www.empireonline.com/movies/news/exclusive-superbob-trailer -soars-online/.

DiPaolo, Marc. *War, Politics, and Superheroes: Ethics and Propaganda in Comics and Film*. Jefferson, NC: McFarland, 2011.

Dittmer, Jason. "American Exceptionalism, Visual Effects, and the Post-9/11 Cinematic Superhero Boom." *Environment and Planning D: Society and Space* 29, no. 1 (2011): 114–30.

——. *Captain America and the Nationalist Superhero: Metaphors, Narratives, and Geopolitics*. Philadelphia: Temple University Press, 2012.

Dyce, Andrew. "David S. Goyer Says *Man of Steel* Will Be 'Realistic' Like Nolan's Batman." *Screenrant.com*, January 10, 2012. http://screenrant.com/superman -man-of-steel-realistic-david-goyer-christopher-nolan-batman/.

Dyer, James. "*Interstellar* Review." *Empire*, April 10, 2013. https://www.empireonline .com/movies/reviews/interstellar-review/.

Eco, Umberto. "The Myth of Superman." *Diacritics* 2, no. 1 (Spring 1972): 14–22.

Ehrlich, David. " 'Joker' Review: For Better or Worse, Superhero Movies Will Never Be the Same." *Indiewire*, August 31, 2019. https://www.indiewire.com/2019/08 /joker-review-joaquin-phoenix-1202170236/.

Elle, Cee Cee. "Wonder Woman Is Not a Feminist Movie." *Medium*, June 19, 2017. https://medium.com/@ceeceeelle/wonder-woman-is-not-a-feminist-movie -6d1071fb980f.

Ellis-Petersen, Hannah. "Malaysia Accused of 'State-Sponsored Homophobia' After LGBT Crackdown." *The Guardian*, August 22, 2018. https://www.theguardian .com/world/2018/aug/22/malaysia-accused-of-state-sponsored-homophobia -after-lgbt-crackdown.

Ellwood, Gregory. "Kevin Feige Says There Will Soon Be at Least Two LGBTQ Heroes in Marvel Universe." *ThePlaylist.net*, June 25, 2018. https://theplaylist.net /kevin-feige-lgbtq-marvel-universe-20180625/.

Ezra, Elizabeth, and Terry Rowden. *Transnational Cinema: The Film Reader*. Abingdon: Routledge, 2006.

Faller, Stephen. "Iron Man's Transcendent Challenges." In *Iron Man and Philosophy*, edited by Mark D. White, 256–64. Hoboken, NJ: Wiley, 2010.

Faludi, Susan. *The Terror Dream: Fear and Fantasy in Post-9/11 America*. Melbourne: Scribe, 2007.

Fleming, Mike, Jr. "Alejandro G. Iñárritu and 'Birdman' Scribes on Hollywood's Superhero Fixation: 'Poison, Cultural Genocide'—Q&A." *Deadline*, October 15, 2014. http://deadline.com/2014/10/birdman-director-alejandro-gonzalez -inarritu-writers-interview-852206/.

——. "George Miller on March Start Date for Next Film, More 'Mad Max', Defending Superheroes as Cinema & the Search for Depth That Makes Movies Like

'Fury Road' Unforgettable." *Deadline.com*, December 6, 2019. https://deadline
.com/2019/12/george-miller-mad-max-fury-road-sequel-superhero-movie
-debate-start-date-three-thousand-years-of-longing-interview-1202802441/
(accessed December 26, 2019).

Flood, Alison. "Superheroes a 'Cultural Catastrophe', Says Comics Guru
Alan Moore." *The Guardian*, January 21, 2014. https://www.theguardian
.com/books/2014/jan/21/superheroes-cultural-catastrophe-alan-moore
-comics-watchmen.

Flores, Emil M. "The Concept of the Superhero in Filipino Films." *Plaridel* 2, no. 2
(August 2005): 23–38.

Frank, Austin. "It Is Your Patriotic Duty to Make Sure Disney's Feminist Propaganda
Piece Captain Marvel Bombs." *Today in Politics*, March 5, 2019. https://tipolitics
.com/2019/03/05/it-is-your-patriotic-duty-to
-make-sure-disneys-feminist-propaganda-piece-captain-marvel-bombs/.

Franich, Darren. "*Incredibles 2* Is a Superheroic Delight, and the Weirdest Pixar Movie
Ever." *Entertainment Weekly*, June 11, 2018. https://ew.com/movies/2018/06/11
/incredibles-2-review/.

Gaine, Vincent M. "Genre and Superheroism: Batman in the New Millennium." In
The 21st Century Superhero: Essays on Gender, Genre, and Globalization in Film,
edited by Richard J. Gray II and Betty Kaklamanidou, 111–128. Jefferson, NC:
MacFarland, 2011.

GLAAD Media Institute. "2018 GLAAD Studio Responsibility Index." 2018. https://www
.glaad.org/files/2018%20GLAAD%20Studio%20Responsibility%20Index.pdf.

Godinez, Henry D. "Why Wonder Woman Is the Perfect Hero for the Trump Era."
Washington Post, June 29, 2017. https://www.washingtonpost.com/news
/posteverything/wp/2017/06/29/why-wonder-woman-is-the-perfect-hero
-for-the-trump-era/.

Gordon, Ian. *Superman: The Persistence of an American Icon*. New Brunswick, NJ: Rutgers
University Press, 2017.

Gray, Richard. Review of *Psychokinesis*. *Reel Bits*, April 28, 2018. https://thereelbits
.com/2018/04/25/review-psychokinesis/.

Gray, Richard J., II, and Betty Kaklamanidou. Introduction to *The 21st Century
Superhero: Essays on Gender, Genre and Globalization in Film*, edited by Richard
J. Gray II and Betty Kaklamanidou, 1–14. Jefferson, NC: MacFarland, 2011.

Green, Darragh, and Kate Roddy. Introduction to *Grant Morrison and the Superhero
Renaissance: Critical Essays*, edited by Darragh Green and Kate Roddy, 1–16.
Jefferson, NC: McFarland, 2015.

Grierson, Tim. Review of *Black Panther*. *Screen Daily*, February 6, 2018. https://www
.screendaily.com/reviews/black-panther-review/5126078.article.

Gunning, Tom. "The Cinema of Attractions: Early Film, Its Spectator, and the Avant-
Garde." In *Early Cinema: Space, Frame, Narrative*, edited by Thomas Elsaesser,
56–62. London: British Film Institute, 1990.

Hagley, Annika. "America's Need for Superheroes Has Led to the Rise of Donald
Trump." *The Guardian*, March 28, 2016. https://www.theguardian.com
/commentisfree/2016/mar/28/america-superheroes-donald-trump-brutal
-comic-book-ideal.

Harwood, John. "Pay Attention to the Man Behind the Curtain: Trump Is No Wizard of
Government." CNBC.com, April 28, 2017. https://www.cnbc.com/2017/04/28
/pay-attention-to-the-man-behind-the-curtain-trump-is-no-wizard-of-government
.html.

Hassler-Forrest, Dan. *Capitalist Superheroes: Caped Crusaders in the Neoliberal Age*.
London: Zero, 2012.

Herbrechter, Stefan. *Posthumanism: A Critical Analysis*. London: Bloomsbury, 2013.

Herhuth, Eric. *Pixar and the Aesthetic Imagination: Animation, Storytelling, and Digital
Culture*. Berkeley: University of California Press, 2017.

Hodges, Michael. "Jodie Foster: 'My Greatest Strength Is What's in My Head.'" *Radio
Times*, January 6, 2018. https://www.radiotimes.com/news/tv/2018–01–06
/jodie-foster-my-greatest-strength-is-whats-in-my-head/.

Hodgeson, Geoffrey. *The Myth of American Exceptionalism*. New Haven, CT: Yale
University Press, 2009.

Hunter, I. Q., and Laraine Porter, eds. *British Comedy Cinema*. New York: Routledge,
2012.

Hyman, David. *Revision and the Superhero Genre*. New York: Palgrave Macmillan,
2017.

"Insider's P.O.V: Jon Drever, Director of *SuperBob*." *Callsheet*, n.d. http://www
.thecallsheet.co.uk/news/insiders-pov-jon-drever-director-superbob. Accessed
September 21, 2019.

Jenkins, Henry. " 'Just Men in Tights': Rewriting Silver Age Comics in an Era of
Multiplicity." In *The Shifting Definitions of Genre: Essays on Labeling Films,
Television Shows, and Media*, edited by Lincoln Geraghty and Mark Jancovich,
229–44. Jefferson, NC: McFarland, 2008.

Jess-Cooke, Carolyn. *Film Sequels: Theory and Practice from Hollywood to Bollywood*.
Edinburgh: Edinburgh University Press, 2009.

Johnson, Tre. "Black Panther Is a Gorgeous, Groundbreaking Celebration of Black Culture." *Vox*, February 23, 2018. https://www.vox.com/culture/2018/2/23 /17028826/black-panther-wakanda-culture-marvel.

Jolin, Dan. "Infographic: Movie Franchise Lexicon." *Empire*, January 9, 2012. http:// www.empireonline.com/movies/features/movie-franchise-lexicon-infographic/.

Karim, Ahnar. "The Marvel Cinematic Universe Is 61% White, but Does That Matter?" *Forbes*, October 10, 2018. https://www.forbes.com/sites/anharkarim/2018 /10/10/the-marvel-cinematic-universe-is-61-white-but-does-that-matter /#fb5d9cc4482e.

Kauer, Raminder. "The Fictions of Science and Cinema in India." In *Routledge Handbook of Indian Cinemas*, edited by K. Moti Gokulsing and Wimal Dissanayake, 282–96. Abingdon: Routledge, 2013.

Kellner, Douglas. *Cinema Wars: Hollywood Film and Politics in the Bush-Cheney Era*. Chichester: Wiley Blackwell, 2010.

Kelly, Emma. "*Avengers: Endgame* Directors Russo Brothers Dragged for Their Attempt at LGBTQ+ Representation." *Metro*, April 29, 2019. https://metro.co.uk/2019 /04/29/avengers-endgame-directors-russo-brothers-dragged-attempt-lgbtq -representation-9335307/.

Khatchatourian, Maana. "Zack Snyder Says Batman and Superman Are Not Like 'Flavor of the Week' Ant-Man." *Variety*, September 10, 2015. http://variety .com/2015/film/news/zack-snyder-batman-superman-not-flavor-of-week -ant-man-1201589800/.

King, Geoff. *Spectacular Narratives: Hollywood in the Age of the Blockbuster*. London: I. B. Tauris, 2000.

Kirkland, Justin. "The Gay Avengers: Endgame Character Is a Half-Baked Attempt at Diversity." *Esquire*, May 1, 2019. https://www.esquire.com/entertainment /movies/a27334096/avengers-endgame-gay-representation/.

Kizu, Kyle. "Fans Are Already Mourning the Avengers." *Hollywood Reporter*, April 19, 2019. https://www.hollywoodreporter.com/heat-vision /avengers-fans-are-mourning-endgame-deaths-1203380.

Klein, Amanda Ann, and R. Barton Palmer, eds. *Cycles, Sequels, Spin-offs, Remakes, and Reboots: Multiplicities in Film and Television*. Austin: University of Texas Press, 2016.

Kolias, George. "Wonder Woman in the Age of Trump." *Huffington Post*, June 9, 2017. https://www.huffingtonpost.com/entry/wonder-woman-in-the-age-of-trump _us_593a46dae4b094fa859f1766.

Kumar, Sujay. "*Krrish 3* Review: What the Bollywood Movie Steals from Superhero Films." *Daily Beast*, August 11, 2013. https://www.thedailybeast.com/krrish-3-review-what-the-bollywood-movie-steals-from-superhero-films.

Langley, Travis, ed. *Batman and Psychology: A Dark and Stormy Knight*. Hoboken, NJ: Wiley, 2012.

Lauzen, Martha M. "It's a Man's (Celluloid) World: Portrayals of Female Characters in the Top 100 Films of 2017." Center for the Study of Women in Television and Film, San Diego State University. 2018. https://womenintvfilm.sdsu.edu/wp-content/uploads/2018/03/2017_Its_a_Mans_Celluloid_World_Report_3.pdf.

Lawrence, John Shelton, and Robert Jewett. *The American Monomyth*. New York: Anchor /Doubleday, 1977.

——. *The Myth of the American Superhero*. Grand Rapids, MI: Eerdmans, 2002.

LeBron, Christopher. "*Black Panther* Is Not the Movie We Deserve." *Boston Review*, February 17, 2018. http://bostonreview.net/race/christopher-lebron-black-panther.

Livingstone, Josephine. "Wonder Woman Is Propaganda." *New Republic*, June 6, 2017. https://newrepublic.com/article/143100/wonder-woman-propaganda.

Lowery, Tim. "Five Lessons Hollywood Learned from Tim Burton's *Batman* (1989)." RottenTomatoes.com, June 23, 2019. https://editorial.rottentomatoes.com/article/five-lessons-hollywood-learned-from-tim-burtons-batman-1989/.

Loayza, Beatrice. "Seen but Not Heard: Why Don't Women Speak in *The Irishman*?" *The Guardian*, November 7, 2019. https://www.theguardian.com/film/2019/nov/07/why-dont-women-speak-in-the-irishman-martin-scorsese-anna-paquin-hollywood.

Maltin, Leonard. "I Wonder What's Wrong with 'Wonder Woman.'" *LeonardMaltin.com*, June 1, 2017. http://leonardmaltin.com/i-wonder-whats-wrong-with-wonder-woman/.

Mandle, Chris. "Donald Trump Tells Naive Child 'I Am Batman' Despite Not Actually Being Batman." *Independent*, August 17, 2015. https://www.independent.co.uk/news/people/donald-trump-tells-naive-child-i-am-batman-despite-not-actually-being-batman-10459503.html.

McArthur, Colin. *Underworld USA*. London: British Film Institute, 1972.

McClelland-Nugent, Ruth. " 'Steve Trevor, Equal?' Wonder Woman in an Era of Second Wave Feminist Critique." In *The Ages of Wonder Woman: Essays on the Amazon Princess in Changing Times*, edited by Joseph Darowski, 136–50. Jefferson, NC: McFarland, 2014.

McClintock, Pamela. "$200 Million and Rising: Hollywood Struggles with Soaring Marketing Costs." *Hollywood Reporter*, July 31, 2014. https://www.hollywoodreporter.com/news/200-million-rising-hollywood-struggles-721818.

McMillan, Graeme. "Why *Guardians of the Galaxy* Is the Riskiest Marvel Film Since *Iron Man*." *Hollywood Reporter*, February 19, 2014. http://www.hollywood reporter.com/heat-vision/why-guardians-galaxy-is-riskiest-681656.

——. "Steven Spielberg Says Superhero Movies Will Go 'the Way of the Western.'" *Hollywood Reporter*, September 2, 2015. http://www.hollywoodreporter.com /heat-vision/steven-spielberg-predicts-superhero-movies-819768.

McSweeney, Terence. *Avengers Assemble! Critical Perspectives on the Marvel Cinematic Universe*. London: Wallflower Press, 2018.

——. *The 'War on Terror' and American Film: 9/11 Frames per Second*. Edinburgh: Edinburgh University Press, 2014.

Medhurst, Andy. "Batman, Deviance, and Camp." In *The Many Lives of the Batman: Critical Approaches to a Superhero and His Media*, edited by Roberta E. Pearson and William Uricchio, 149–63. London: Routledge, 1991.

Meinel, Dietmar. *Pixar's America: The Re-Animation of American Myths and Symbols*. New York: Palgrave Macmillan, 2018.

Melamid, Alex. "Blame Donald Trump's Rise on the Avant-Garde Movement." *Time*, May 12, 2017. http://time.com/4777118/avant-garde-koons-trump/.

Miliora, Maria T. *The Scorsese Psyche on Screen: Roots of Themes and Characters in the Films*. Jefferson, NC: McFarland, 2015.

Miller, Cynthia J., ed. *Too Bold for the Box Office: The Mockumentary from Big Screen to Small*. Lanham, MD: Scarecrow, 2012.

Mirrlees, Tanner. "How to Read *Iron Man*: The Economics, Politics, and Ideology of an Imperial Film Commodity." *Cineaction* 92, no. 1 (2014): 4–11.

Mock, Brentlin. "*Black Panther* Marks Milestone in Black Culture's Impact on Hollywood." NBCNews.com, February 11, 2018. https://www.nbcnews.com /pop-culture/movies/black-panther-marks-milestone-black-culture-s-impact -hollywood-n846891.

Monbiot, George. "Neoliberalism—the Ideology at the Root of All Our Problems." *The Guardian*, April 15, 2016. https://www.theguardian.com/books/2016/apr /15/neoliberalism-ideology-problem-george-monbiot.

Morrison, Grant. *SuperGods: Our World in the Age of the Superhero*. London: Random House, 2011.

Muller, Christine. "Power, Choice, and September 11 in *The Dark Knight*." In *The 21st Century Superhero: Essays on Gender, Genre, and Globalization in Film*, edited by Richard J. Gray and Betty Kaklamanidou, 46–59. Jefferson, NC: MacFarland, 2011.

Murray, Chris. *The British Superhero*. Jackson: University of Mississippi Press, 2017.

Nama, Adilifu. *Super Black: American Pop Culture and Black Superheroes*. Austin: University of Texas Press, 2011.

Nochimson, Martha P. *World on Film: An Introduction*. Oxford: Wiley-Blackwell, 2011.

Obikili, Nonso "Toxic Economics and Politics: The *Black Panther* Edition." *Nonso Obikili's Blog*, February 23, 2018. https://nonsoobikili.wordpress.com/2018/02/23/toxic-economics-and-politics-the-black-panther-edition/.

O'Brien, Daniel. *Black Masculinity on Film: Native Sons and White Lies*. New York: Palgrave Macmillan, 2017.

O'Hehir, Andrew. "*The Dark Knight Rises*: Christopher Nolan's Evil Masterpiece." *Salon.com*, July 18, 2012. http://www.salon.com/2012/07/18/the_dark_knight_rises_christopher_nolans_evil_masterpiece/.

Oller, Jacob. "Shazam's Suit Cost Over $1 Million Dollars—and They Made 10 of Them." Syfy.com, January 15,2019. https://www.syfy.com/syfywire/shazams-suit-cost-over-1-million-dollars-and-they-made-10-of-them.

O'Neill, Denis. Introduction to *Batman and Psychology: A Dark and Stormy* Knight, edited by Travis Langley, 1–4. Hoboken, NJ: Wiley, 2012.

Pearson, Ben. "*Logan* Is a Western Because of Audiences' Exhaustion with 'Formulaic' Superhero Movies, Says Director." *Gamesradar*, March 1, 2017. https://www.gamesradar.com/logan-is-a-western-because-of-audiences-exhaustion-with-formulaic-superhero-movies-says-director/.

Pearson, Roberta, William Uricchio, and Will Brooker, eds. *Many More Lives of the Batman*. London: British Film Institute, 2015.

Pennington, Ron. Review of *Batman*. *Hollywood Reporter*, June 23, 1989. https://www.hollywoodreporter.com/news/batman-thrs-1989-review-801339.

Pheasant-Kelly, Francis. *Fantasy Film Post 9/11*. New York: Palgrave MacMillan, 2013.

Pitts, Leonard, Jr. "*Black Panther* a Watershed in Cultural History of African Americans." *Miami Herald*, February 15, 2018. https://www.miamiherald.com/opinion/opn-columns-blogs/leonard-pitts-jr/article200350754.html.

Pollard, Tom. *Hollywood 9/11: Superheroes, Supervillains, and Super Disasters*. Boulder, CO: Paradigm, 2011.

Powell, Mark. "The Radical Politics of *Black Panther*." *Spectator*, February 26, 2018. https://www.spectator.com.au/2018/02/the-radical-politics-of-black-panther/.

Price, David. *The Pixar Touch: The Making of a Company*. New York: Vintage, 2009.

Prince, Stephen. *Firestorm: American Film in the Age of Terrorism*. New York: Columbia University Press, 2009.

Pritchard, Tiffany. " 'Scorsese Wasn't Thinking Correctly' Says Marvel Cinematographer Dante Spinotti." *Screendaily*, December 1, 2019. https://www.screendaily.com /news/scorsese-wasnt-thinking-correctly-says-marvel-cinematographer-dante -spinotti/5145209.article.

Prouix, Natalie. "Is *Black Panther* a 'Defining Moment' for the United States—and Particularly for Black America?" *New York Times*, March 1, 2018. https://www .nytimes.com/2018/03/01/learning/is-black-panther-a-defining-moment-for -the-united-states-and-particularly-for-black-america.html.

Purse, Lisa. *Contemporary Action Cinema*. Edinburgh: Edinburgh University Press, 2011.

Rawden, Jessica. "How Much Pirates of the Caribbean Movies Have Shelled Out Just for Snacks." Cinemablend.com, May 28, 2017. https://www.cinemablend .com/news/1664249/how-much-pirates-of-the-caribbean-movies-have-shelled -out-just-for-snacks.

Reynolds, Richard. *Superheroes: A Modern Mythology*. Jackson, MS: University Press of Mississippi, 1992.

Ridgely, Charlie. "Brad Bird Reveals Why Each 'Incredibles' Character Has Their Specific Power." *Comicbook.com*, April 16, 2018. https://comicbook.com /movies/2018/04/15/why-incredibles-have-specific-powers-pixar-brad-bird/.

Rivera, Joshua. "*Logan* Looks Like the Superhero Western We All Need to See." *GQ*, January 19, 2017. https://www.gq.com/story/logan-looks-like-the-superhero -western-we-all-need-to-see.

Roberts, Garyn. "Understanding the Sequential Art of Comic Strips and Comic Books and Their Descendants in the Early Years of the New Millennium." *Journal of American Culture* 27, no. 2 (2004): 210–17.

Rojek, Chris. *Celebrity*. London: Reaktion, 2001.

Russo, Vito. *The Celluloid Closet: Homosexuality in the Movies*. New York: Harper & Row, 1981.

Ryan, Tom. "In Defence of Big, Expensive Films." *The Age*, July 14, 2005. http://www .theage.com.au/news/film/defending-the-blockbuster /2005/07/14/1120934352863.html.

Salkowitz, Rob. "*Batman v Superman* Is A Blockbuster for the Trump Era." *Forbes*, March 28, 2016. https://www.forbes.com/sites/robsalkowitz/2016/03/28 /batman-v-superman-is-a-blockbuster-for-the-trump-era/#530f3cb94cb6.

Sarmiento, Wlad. "The Standard Badass Superhero of Captain Marvel." *Chicago Maroon*. March 21, 2019. https://www.chicagomaroon.com/article/2019/3/21 /standard-badass-superhero-captain-marvel/.

Saunders, Ben. *Do Gods Wear Capes? Spirituality, Fantasy, and Superheroes*. London: Bloomsbury, 2011.

Schwerdtfeger, Conner. "Is Michael B. Jordan's Killmonger Marvel's Best Villain Yet?" *Cinemablend.com*, February 16, 2018. https://www.cinemablend.com/news /2312522/is-michael-b-jordans-killmonger-marvels-best-villain-yet.

Scorsese, Martin. "I Said Marvel Movies Aren't Cinema. Let Me Explain." *New York Time*, November 4 2019. https://www.nytimes.com/2019/11/04/opinion/martin -scorsese-marvel.html.

Sharf, Zack. "Terry Gilliam Sounds Off on Superhero Movies: 'I Hate Them. It's Bullshit. Come On, Grow Up!'" *Indiewire.com*, June 26, 2018. https://www.indiewire.com /2018/06/terry-gilliam-superhero-movies-hatred-bullshit-1201971699/.

Shoard, Catherine. "Ethan Hawke: Superhero Movies Are Overrated." *The Guardian*, August 27, 2018. https://www.theguardian.com/film/2018/aug/27/ethan-hawke -superhero-movies-are-overrated-logan.

——. "*Son of Saul*'s László Nemes: 'Our Civilisation Is Preparing for Its Own Destruction.'" *The Guardian*, May 10, 2019. https://www.theguardian.com/film/2019/may/10 /son-of-sauls-laszlo-nemes-our-civilisation-is-preparing-for-its-own-destruction.

Sieczkowski, Cavan. "Ian McKellen Took *X-Men* Role Because of Gay Rights Parallel." *Huffington Post*, February 27, 2014. https://www.huffingtonpost.co.uk/2014/02/27 /ian-mckellen-x-men-gay_n_4865739.html.

Simons, Paula. "Get Us Out from Under, Wonder Woman." *Edmonton Journal*, June 2, 2017. https://edmontonjournal.com/opinion/columnists/paula-simons-get-us -out-from-under-wonder-woman.

6ABC News. "Philly Audiences Find Deeper Meaning in *Black Panther*." February 16, 2018. YouTube video. https://www.youtube.com /watch?v=b4kEEpnfLrl.

Slotkin, Richard. *Regeneration Through Violence*. Norman: University of Oklahoma Press, 1973.

Smith, Anna. "How *Incredibles 2* Goes to Work for the Feminist Superhero." *The Guardian*, June 28, 2018. https://www.theguardian.com/film/2018/jun/28 /incredibles-2-feminism-animation.

Smith, Iain Robert. *The Hollywood Meme: Transnational Adaptations in World Cinema*. Edinburgh: Edinburgh University Press, 2018.

Smith, Jamil. "The Revolutionary Power of *Black Panther*." *Time*, February 11, 2019. http://time.com/black-panther/.

Smith, Stacy L., Marc Choueiti, Katherine Pieper, Ariana Case, and Angel Choi. "Inequality in 1,100 Popular Films: Examining Portrayals of Gender, Race/Ethnicity, LGBT, and Disability from 2007 to 2017." Annenberg Foundation and USC Annenberg Inclusion Institute, July 2018, http://assets.uscannenberg.org /docs/inequality-in-1100-popular-films.pdf..

Smith, Stacy L., Marc Choueiti, Dr. Katherine Pieper, Kevin Yao, Ariana Case & Angel Cho. "Inequality in 1,200 Popular Films: Examining Portrayals of Gender, Race/ Ethnicity, LGBTQ & Disability from 2007 to 2018." Media, Diversity, and Social Change Initiative, USC Annenberg. 2019. .

Smith, Stacy L., Katherine Pieper, and Marc Choueiti. "Inclusion in the Director's Chair? Gender, Race, & Age of Film Directors Across 1,000 Films from 2007– 2016." Media, Diversity, and Social Change Initiative, USC Annenberg. 2017. http://annenberg.usc.edu/pages/~/media /MDSCI/Inclusion%20in%20the%20Directors%20Chair%202117%20Final. ashxhttp://annenberg.usc.edu/pages/~/media/MDSCI/Inclusion%20in %20the%20Directors%20Chair%202117%20Final.ashx.

Smith, Stacy L., Katherine Pieper, Marc Choueiti, Traci Gillig, Carmen Lee, and Dylan DeLuca. "Inequality in 700 Popular Films: Examining Portrayals of Gender, Race, & LGBT Status from 2007 to 2014." Media, Diversity, and Social Change Initiative, USC Annenberg. 2015. http://annenberg.usc.edu/pages/~/media/MDSCI /Inequality%20in %20700%20Popular%20Films%208215%20Final%20for%20Posting.ashx.

Smith, Stacy L., Katherine Pieper, Marc Choueiti, Traci Gillig, Carmen Lee, and Dylan DeLuca. "Inequality in 800 Popular Films: Examining Portrayals of Gender, Race, & LGBT Status from 2007 to 2015." Media, Diversity, and Social Change Initiative, USC Annenberg. 2016. http://annenberg.usc.edu/pages/~/media/MDSCI/Dr %20Stacy%20L%20Smith%20Inequality%20in%20800%20Films%20FINAL.ashx.

Spencer, Keith. "Peak Superhero? Not Even Close: How One Movie Genre Became the Guiding Myth of Neoliberalism," *Salon*, April 28, 2018. https://www.salon .com/2018/04/28/how-superhero-films-became-the-guiding-myth-of-neoliberalism/.

Stam, Robert. *Film Theory: An Introduction*. Malden, UK: Blackwell, 2000.

Steinem, Gloria. "Wonder Woman" (1972). In *The Superhero Reader*, edited by Charles Hatfield, Jeet Heer, and Kent Worcester, 203–10. Jackson: University of Mississippi Press, 2013.

Svetkey, Benjamin. "Q+A Director's Chair." *Entertainment Weekly*, July 25, 2008. http://www.ew.com/ew/article/0,,20215252,00.html.

Thomas, Shibu. "TV Writer Seeks Stay on *Ra.One*." *Times of India*, October 21, 2011. https://timesofindia.indiatimes.com/city/mumbai/TV-writer-seeks-stay-on -Ra-One/articleshow/10434305.cms.

Togina. "Brooklyn." Archiveofourown.com. May 21, 2014. https://archiveofourown
.org/works/1669439.

Toh, Justine. "The Tools and Toys of (the) War (on Terror): Consumer Desire, Military
Fetish, and Regime Change in *Batman Begins*." In *Reframing 9/11: Film, Popular
Culture, and the 'War on Terror,'* edited by Jeff Birkenstein, Anna Froula, and Karen
Randell, 127–39. London: Continuum, 2010.

Tseng, Ada. "The Complex History of Asian Americans in Movies, from the Silent Era
to *Crazy Rich Asians*." *Washington Post*, August 8, 2018. https://www
.washingtonpost.com/entertainment/the-complex-history-of-asian-americans
-in-movies-from-the-silent-era-to-crazy-rich-asians/2018/08/08/77bc4176-9666
-11e8-810c-5fa705927d54_story.html.

Vishnevetsky, Ignatiy. "The Entertaining and Ambitious *Black Panther* Breaks from
the Marvel Formula." *A.V. Club*, February 14, 2018. https://www.avclub.com
/the-entertaining-and-ambitious-black-panther-breaks-fro-1822976016.

Wainer, Alex M. *Soul of the Dark Knight: Batman as Mythic Figure in Comics and Film.*
Jefferson, NC: MacFarland, 2014.

Wallace, Carvell. "Why *Black Panther* Is a Defining Moment for Black America."
New York Times Magazine, February 12, 2018. https://www.nytimes.com/2018
/02/12/magazine/why-black-panther-is-a-defining-moment-for-black-america.html.

Wallace, Richard. *Mockumentary Comedy: Performing Authenticity.* New York:
Palgrave Macmillan, 2019.

Weiner, Robert G. "Sequential Art and Reality: Yes, Virginia, There Is a Spider-Man."
International Journal of Comic Art 11, no. 1 (Spring 2009): 457–477.

Wertham, Frederic. *Seduction of the Innocent.* New York: Rinehart, 1954.

Westbrooke, Caroline. "There's Going to Be an LGBT Superhero in the Marvel Cinematic
Universe." *Metro*, June 30, 2015. https://metro.co.uk/2015/06/30/just-when
-the-marvel-cinematic-universe-introduce-an-lgbtq-character-kevin-feige-says
-itll-be-within-a-decade-5272298/.

Whitaker, Matthew C. *Icons of Black America: Breaking Barriers and Crossing
Boundaries.* Santa Barbara, CA: ABC-CLIO, 2011.

White, Armond. "What Does a Wonder Womanchild Want?" *National Review*, June 2,
2017. https://www.nationalreview.com/2017/06/wonder-woman-pc-heroine-lacks
-passion-complexity/.

Williams, Zoe. "Why *Wonder Woman* Is a Masterpiece of Subversive Feminism."
The Guardian, June 5, 2017. https://www.theguardian.com/lifeandstyle/2017
/jun/05/why-wonder-woman-is-a-masterpiece-of-subversive-feminism.

Wittmer, Carrie. "The Top 22 Marvel Cinematic Universe Villains, Ranked from Worst to Best." *Business Insider*, July 23, 2018. https://www.businessinsider.com/marvel -cinematic-universe-villains-ranked-from-worst-to-best-2018-2.

Womack, Ytasha. *Afrofuturism: The World of Black Sci-Fi and Fantasy Culture*. Chicago: Lawrence Hill, 2013.

Wong, Eugene Franklin. *On Visual Media Racism: Asians in the American Motion Pictures*. New York: Arno, 1978.

Xing, Jun. *Asian America Through the Lens: History, Representations, and Identity*. New York: Altamira, 1998.

Zakarin, Jordan. "David Cronenberg Slams Superhero Films, Calls 'Dark Knight Rises' Boring." *Hollywood Reporter*, August 15, 2012. http://www.hollywoodreporter .com/heat-vision/david-cronenberg-slams-superhero-films-batman-boring -362780.

Zainul, Emir. "Website Blocking in Malaysia Has Reduced Online Piracy, Says Film Makers Body." *Edge Markets*, October 10, 2017. http://www.theedgemarkets .com/article/website-blocking-malaysia-has-reduced-online-piracy-says-film -makers-body.

Zeldin-O'Neill, Sophie, and Jonross Swaby. ' "There Are Gay Characters in the Marvel Universe': Guardians of the Galaxy Vol 2 Cast and Crew Interviewed—Video." *The Guardian*, May 1, 2017. https://www.theguardian.com/film/video/2017/may/01 /gay-characters-marvel-guardians-of-the-galaxy-vol-2-chris-pratt-karen-gillan.

Žižek, Slavoj. "Quasi Duo Fantasias: A Straussian Reading of *Black Panther*." *Los Angeles Review of Books*, March 3, 2018. https://lareviewofbooks.org/article/quasi-duo -fantasias-straussian-reading-black-panther/.

INDEX

Page numbers in *italics* indicate photos.

SHORT CUTS

INTRODUCTIONS TO FILM STUDIES